Panfishing

Panfishing

Complete Angler's Library™
North American Fishing Club
Minneapolis, Minnesota

Panfishing

Copyright © 1991, North American Fishing Club

Library of Congress Catalog Card Number 91-60047
ISBN 0-914697-37-4

Printed in U.S.A.
        3   4   5   6   7   8   9

The North American Fishing Club
offers a line of hats for fishermen.
For information, write:
        North American Fishing Club
        P.O. Box 3403
        Minneapolis, MN 55343

Contents

Acknowledgments 1
About The Authors 3
Foreword 9

The Popular Panfish
1 The Fun And Romance Of Panfishing 14
2 Panfishing Equipment 20
3 Baits And Lures 42
4 The Ultimate Panfish Boat 58

Sunfish
5 Sunfishing's Big Three 70
6 The Other Sunfish 84
7 Finding And Catching Sunfish 98
8 Catching Sunfish In Special Situations 110

Crappies
9 Meet The Crappie 126
10 Finding And Catching Crappies 138
11 Special Situations For Crappies 154

Yellow Perch
12 All About Yellow Perch 170
13 Finding And Catching Perch 180
14 Special Situations For Perch 194

Other Panfish
15 White Bass And Yellow Bass 208
16 Rock Bass And Warmouths 216
17 Bullheads And Other Catfish 226

Ice Fishing For Perch
18 Getting Equipped For Ice Fishing 240
19 Ice Fishing Tactics For Sunfish, Crappies 254
20 Ice Fishing For Perch 266

Acknowledgments

The North American Fishing Club would like to thank everyone who made this book possible.

Guides Skip Davis and Wayne Hughes and biologists Mark Oliver and Jeff Boxrucker provided technical information to the authors.

Photographs were provided by the authors. Soc Clay, Jim Low, Jay Strangis, Paul DeMarchi and Ken Clary of Crappiethon USA contributed additional photos. Wildlife artist Virgil Beck created the cover art; artists David Rottinghaus and John A. (Buzz) Buczynski created all illustrations.

A special thanks to the fishing club's publication staff for their efforts to complete this book: Editor and Publisher Mark LaBarbera, Managing Editor Steve Pennaz, Managing Editor Ron Larsen, Editorial Assistant Colleen Ferguson and Layout Artist Dean Peters. Thanks also to Vice President of Product Marketing Mike Vail, Marketing Manager Linda Kalinowski and Marketing Project Coordinator Laura Resnik.

About The Authors

R ichard Martin began his fishing at roughly the age of six, and
his first quarry was creek minnows using bread and a willow
pole. Since then he has become a world traveler who has fished for
cod off Nova Scotia, for sea trout around Louisiana oil rigs, and for
salmon in salty waters around Vancouver Island. But he still loves
perch fishing. Whenever time permits, he'll head for Lake Erie to
try for a limit, or seek similar success on a mesotrophic lake such as
Minnesota's Mille Lacs, or in a Lake Michigan bay. Anywhere
good-sized perch can be found.

His educational background also indicates his interest in fish.
He has a bachelor of science degree in biology from Ohio Univer-
sity and a master's degree in zoology, specializing in fish, from
Ohio State University.

Richard has been an outdoor writer since 1965. He writes a
column each week for four Ohio newspapers, and is on the staff of
several more tabloid publications. He has written magazine articles on a variety of outdoor subjects, and had them published in
magazines from *Outdoor Life* and *Sports Afield* to *Game And Fish*
and *Walleye Magazine*. Over 3,000 articles have carried his byline
so far, and he's supplemented his tally with three books, one of
them on Lake Erie fishing.

Richard, having passed the 50-year mark now, says his out-
door-writing years have been good ones. A patient, long-suffering

wife, Jane, and two grown children, Jill and Scott, still like to fish. "Teaching those youngsters the joys of fishing gave me some of my happiest trips," he says.

Richard is a member of the Outdoor Writers Association of America (OWAA) and the Outdoor Writers of Ohio (OWO), and has served as vice president of OWO. He has received a number of awards for excellence in both newspaper and magazine writing, topped by a major tribute from Maryland when he was named "Travel Writer of the Year" for a series of articles on Maryland's eastern shore.

His plans for the future include "more books, more newspaper and magazine articles and more travel. I love to travel around the North American continent learning how an Eskimo catches Arctic char or a Cape Hatteras surfer casts for bluefish. And I love heading overseas to watch or join English anglers trying for tench or German fishermen working for a catch of eels. There are so many types of fishing, and so many places to do it that there's always a new challenge, a new place to go. And I plan to meet that challenge, and go there."

Full-time outdoor writer/photographer Gary Nelson has fished for about 35 years. Nelson is a multispecies angler, but he spends most of his fishing time now pursuing crappies. Fishing for crappies in about two dozen states, from Washington state to Florida, he has caught and released as many as 400 to 500 in a day.

A professional journalist for about 15 years, Gary's articles and photos have appeared in about 70 magazines including all the major outdoor magazines as well as specialty magazines for crappie anglers. He's author of the column, "Experiments in Crappie Fishing," and his photographs on crappie fishing have appeared on a number of magazine covers. A columnist and field editor for vari-

ous publications, he's an active member of the Outdoor Writers Association of America and a fellow member of the North American Fishing Club. Nelson is a graduate of Clark College (Washington State) where he majored in journalism.

A native of Minnesota, Gary has also lived and fished many years in the South. He and his family live near Bull Shoals Lake on the Arkansas-Missouri border.

Gary enjoys crappie fishing because they are found almost any place in the country and are one of the most challenging fish. Crappies also are one of the most exciting catches for Gary. "Just the other day I was fishing with my wife at a local dock and I let out an extremely loud scream," he said. "My wife thought something was drastically wrong, but I was screaming because I had hooked a crappie."

Gary says every time he fishes for specklesides is like it was the first time. "One of the the nice things about crappie fishing is it can be considered action fishing," he said. "If one bites, it is possible 20 could bite."

Gary strongly believes in the conservation of crappie. On lakes where crappie are overfished, Gary will "catch and release." On the other hand, if a lake is overpopulated with crappie, Gary keeps and eats what he catches.

"Crappie are one of the best-eating fish in the world and they are also one of the most exciting to catch," he said. "But what I like most is the challenge." He pursues the secrets of catching crappie on a day-by-day basis. He is so devoted to crappie fishing he now writes his own outdoor newsletter entitled, "The Crappie Fisherman."

A t the ripe old age of six, sitting on the bank of an uncle's east Arkansas farm pond, wielding a freshly cut, green cane pole and a coffee can full of worms dug from beneath a backyard pecan tree, Keith Sutton was introduced to the sport of panfishing by his grandmother, Vivian. "We caught bluegills, redears, crappies and green sunfish," Keith says. "Nothing big. Nothing special. But it was a day I've never forgotten. It was the beginning of a lifelong love of panfishing."

Now, more than a quarter of a century later, Keith is an old hand at panfishing. His passion for the sport has taken him to

blue-ribbon panfish waters in more than 20 different states. He admits he has much more to learn, but already he possesses special insights about panfishing garnered through years of on-the-water research and countless hours of discussions with biologists, researchers and expert anglers. Much of what he has learned is shared in this book, so you, too, can experience the many thrills this popular sport has to offer.

In 1985, after working as park naturalist, ranger and Boy Scout executive, Keith began a career with the Arkansas Game & Fish Commission where he is in charge of publications production and serves as assistant editor for *Arkansas Game & Fish Magazine*. During his tenure with the Commission, he has authored several books and special publications about fishing and the outdoors, including *An Angler's Guide to Arkansas Fish* and *The Angler's Guide to Arkansas Game & Fish Commission Lakes*. The latter publication was honored by the Association of Conservation Information the year of its publication as the best special publications effort by a state wildlife agency.

Keith is also a prolific free-lance writer and photographer, well-known in his native South. After earning a degree in wildlife management at Arkansas State University in 1978, he wrote and illustrated a natural history column for the *Wynne Shopper* newspaper, a small Arkansas weekly. He entered the field of magazine writing in 1980 when his first story appeared in *Fins & Feathers*. Since that time, he has authored more than 500 feature articles that have been published in *Field & Stream, Petersen's Hunting, Crappie World, Bassin', Game & Fish Publications*, and many other state, regional and national periodicals. His works as an award-winning photographer have been featured in a broad spectrum of books, magazines, newspapers and calendars.

Sutton is a respected and recognized member of the outdoor writers' fraternity. He served two terms as president of the Arkansas Outdoor Press Association and is an active member of the Outdoor Writers Association of America and the Southeast Outdoor Press Association. He was raised in Cherry Valley, Arkansas, and now resides near Benton, less than a mile from the Saline River, one of Arkansas' finest panfish streams.

Keith's three sons—Joshua, Matthew and Jared—are all ardent anglers and favorite subjects for his stories and photographs. His wife Vicki, he says, "is the most understanding of fishing widows. Had it not been for her love and encouragement, my fishing sojourns in Arkansas and throughout the country would be but a dream."

Of all the species of panfish described in this book, only one—the Roanoke bass, a type of rock bass—has managed to elude him. That's a situation he intends to remedy as soon as possible. After all, Keith asks, "How many people can say they've made a Grand Slam on panfish?"

Foreword

The other day, a business acquaintance visited NAFC headquarters. After taking care of the business at hand, the conversation (of course) turned to fishing. This particular individual had a number of exotic fishing trips planned for later in the year, and his excitement grew as he described each one. He would start the year with four days in sunny Florida fishing the flats with one of the top guides in the Keys. Then, when the weather warmed up a bit in northern Canada, he would steal away to a great fly-in lake for a week of exciting action. A month or so after that, it was time to head south again for some off-shore marlin fishing.

"What are your plans?" he inquired.

"Nothing as exciting as you," I answered. "I have a salmon and steelhead trip to the Great Lakes planned for early June, and there's a possibility I'll take a fly-in trip to northern Ontario for trophy pike in September. But right now I'm having a ball catching bluegills on a little lake near my house. It has been nothing to catch a limit in a couple hours the past few days."

"Bluegills?" he answered in obvious disgust. "I used to have fun catching them when I was a kid, but I don't waste my time on them anymore."

"Waste your time?" I shot back. "When did catching fish become a 'waste of time' for you?"

"Let me rephrase that," he replied. "Panfish are great for beginning anglers, but they're too easy to catch for anyone who has been at this game for more than a couple years."

"So you're saying anyone who enjoys panfishing is a rank beginner?"

"Well, no. But let's face it, they're not as exciting to catch as an 8-pound bass or a big walleye."

"Maybe for you, but there are plenty of other anglers out there who would rather catch a basket full of crappies than wait all day for one fish. Is it wrong to enjoy fishing panfish because they can be easy to catch? I don't think so."

I can't for the life of me understand why some anglers feel the need to belittle panfish and panfishing. It's such an all-out fun sport that, often, can be as challenging as outwitting the biggest bass. And for those who want more out of their fishing than just size, panfishing can lead you back to what fishing is suppose to be—fun and relaxing.

The NAFC staff wrestled with a number of questions before deciding to add a panfish book to our popular Complete Angler's Library ™ series. The biggest question was whether there was a perceived need for such a book. There is a common misconception that panfishing is easy, and anyone with a hook, line and sinker can catch their limit of these plentiful fish in a short time. While this happens often enough for rumors to have started, there are times when panfishing can get downright tough, and only those anglers who know the little tricks and techniques that open the mouths of lethargic panfish will enjoy good, consistent success.

In the end, the decision to do this book was easy. Few anglers enjoy consistent panfishing success, especially those of us who fish a variety of panfish species. There is too much to learn in a lifetime about the wonderful pan-sized fish that inhabit our fertile waters. Much more than most anglers realize.

We made it our goal to produce a book that would help all NAFC members improve their panfishing skills. The first step in achieving that goal was to identify all the major panfish species. We wanted to make sure we didn't leave any stones unturned. In these pages you will find the best tactics and tips for catching all types of panfish, including sunfish, crappies, perch and white and yellow bass. There are even tips for catching bullhead.

The second step was to identify and hire the top panfish writers to do the book. This was a difficult task. Although a number of writers cover panfish, few specialize in them. But three stood out, and after talking with Keith Sutton, Richard Martin and Gary Nelson, we knew we had put together a team of experts that could do a panfishing book that NAFC members would truly appreciate.

Expect a lot from this book. It's going to show you there is more to panfishing than you ever thought possible. If you doubt this claim, ask yourself these three questions:

- Can I consistently find and catch crappies during the summer months after they have left the shallows?
- When is the last time I caught a bluegill that weighed more than a pound? Have I ever caught a bluegill that weighed a pound or more?
- How long does it take to fillet a 5-gallon bucket full of jumbo perch? Bluegills? Crappies?

This little self-test, if answered honestly, proves panfishing is no piece of cake.

If you are a panfishing critic like the gentleman mentioned at the beginning, I urge you to take a second look at panfish. They can be as challenging as any other fish that swims, or easy enough to forgive your mistakes. In either case, enjoyable fishing awaits you.

Steve Pennaz
Executive Director
North American Fishing Club

The Popular
Panfish

1

The Fun And Romance Of Panfishing

Panfishing. The word means different things to different people. But for nearly all anglers, it is a word that conjures up special memories. For NAFC members, it inspires thoughts of childhood fishing trips with friends or relatives, dunking worms in a farm pond or lazy creek, and thrilling to the pulse of scrappy sunfish dashing to and fro at the end of the line. Some remember dogwoods blooming along the lakeshore as big calico crappies were pulled one after another from a brushpile hidey-hole. Others think back to frosty winter days ice fishing for perch, or a mid-summer's morning spent casting spoons to surfacing white bass, or that just-right autumn afternoon when the rock bass snatched up every fly thrown their way.

Yes, looking back over years of angling, many anglers find that no memories are so cherished and revered as those of special moments spent panfishing.

Some might say the largemouth bass, with its hit-'em-hard, tail-walking fighting style, is the finest sportfish swimming in American waters. Kindred accolades could be given to the acrobatic trout, the heavyweight striped bass, the crafty walleye, or numerous other gamefish, each of which holds a special attraction for its own group of fanatical devotees. When all is said and done, though, panfish still come out on top as a favorite target of America's fishing force.

According to one recent national survey, panfish (including true sunfish, crappies, yellow perch, white and yellow bass, rock

Hefty sunfish like this green sunfish/bluegill hybrid flourish in small farm ponds where an abundant species, the bluegill, and a scarce species, the green sunfish, will crossbreed.

The Fun And Romance Of Panfishing

The glory of fishing for sunnies is that the feisty ones will take baits which are practically their own size. This little longear did just that, smacking a diving crankbait.

bass, warmouths and bullheads) rank above all others in terms of popularity. This study indicated there were more than 31 million panfishermen 16 years old and older who spent more than 592 million days pursuing their favored quarry. In other words, over 78 percent of America's 39.8 million freshwater anglers age 16 and up panfished, compared with 16.2 million (41 percent) who fished for black bass (largemouth and smallmouth), the second most popular group of fish. A survey of NAFC members showed 79 percent fished for all types of bass, but panfish were a strong second at 65 percent.

Why all this attention and devotion? Well, there are several good reasons.

Panfish will gobble up an astounding variety of baits and lures—crickets, worms, grass shrimp, chicken liver, maggots, minnows, mussels, jigs, crankbaits, spinners, flies, poppers, spoons, plastic worms and even catfish stinkbait. Most are not especially wary, and some will even forgive the most slipshod angling techniques. They fight like blue blazes for their size, are tops on the dinner table, and there are umpteen-jillion of them in nearly every lake, river, creek and farm pond in the country. Nowhere in

Complete Angler's Library

the continental U.S. is one more than a short drive away from a body of water well populated with panfish.

If you need further qualifications to satisfy critics, consider that panfish can be caught with practically any kind of tackle—everything from a high-dollar, high-tech, ultra-light spinning rig to a plain ol' stick rigged with baling twine and a safety pin. Panfishing can be enjoyed year-round and is a great way to introduce kids to the joys of angling. Many accomplished anglers mastered the basics of fishing as a youngster catching bullheads in a farm pond or crappies in a small lake. Best of all, panfish are a source of bald-faced, indisputable, all-out fun. Fishing for them is one of the most enjoyable pastimes available to America's many outdoor recreationists.

Surprisingly, all these characteristics may be responsible for the noticeable *unpopularity* of panfish in some circles.

The common reasons are: "Eat anything." "Easy to catch." "Found everywhere." "Unwary." "Heck, panfish are kids' fish." "Not for me, thank you."

That's the lamentable conclusion many of us reach once we've hooked our first big bass or outwitted a trout with a hand-tied fly. All of a sudden, we become "The Uppity Angler," suave and sophisticated, and panfish join the ranks of the unworthy for the very reasons listed above.

Fortunately, for most true sportsmen, this is just a passing phase, and there comes a day when our fishing endeavors take on new meaning.

Most of us started our angling careers at a stage where all that mattered was catching lots of fish and having lots of fun. Panfish fit the bill.

Later, we passed through a stage in which the status of the fish was the key to fulfillment. Fishing didn't have much meaning unless we caught our limits of bass or trout or stripers or other "meaningful" fish—the bigger the better.

But, finally, thank goodness, most anglers come to realize that fishing can be an end unto itself. It clears the mind and soothes the soul. Catching big fish, lots of fish, may still be part of the objective, but it's no longer the ultimate object of our trips afield. We don't have to catch limits to enjoy a day out. We don't even have to keep any fish. We're out to have fun, to relax, to take in the outdoors. And once again, the simpler pleasures are enough to satisfy.

While some anglers might claim that sunfish are just for kids, what angler in his right mind would pass up the kind of fun these kids had in catching a mess of bluegills and redears.

Complete Angler's Library

It's at this point that many of us rediscover the fun and romance of fishing for panfish.

Remember when you thought that catching panfish was the greatest thing going? Maybe it's time to recapture that feeling. If you agree, then read on. There's plenty here to rekindle your interest in panfishing.

If you're a stranger to the sport, one who hasn't yet experienced the immeasurable joys panfishing has to offer, this book is for you as well. We'll introduce you to bluegills, redear sunfish, redbreast sunfish, crappies, yellow perch, white bass, yellow bass, rock bass, warmouths, bullheads and other popular panfish. Then, we'll give you the information you need to enjoy a productive outing for these down-to-earth, dependable sportfish.

If you can't go fishing right now, then by all means, do the next best thing. Sit back in your easy chair, relax and slip into the world of panfish, America's fishing favorites.

2

Panfishing Equipment

Certainly, one of the attractions of panfishing is that the gear required to take nice stringers of these fish can be as simple or as sophisticated as the individual angler cares to have it. Panfish, although scrappy for their size, still are small enough that an angler is not going to use real heavy-duty equipment, but that doesn't mean that there aren't a lot of choices to be made in the way of equipment. Here's a brief look at the types of equipment you can use to further enhance your panfishing adventures.

Casting Rods

Casting rods are by far the most popular for panfish, and many anglers use nothing else. Casting rods work, and work well. However, their shorter length is a disadvantage in weeds or drowned timber. Perch fishermen like them because they're great for making longer casts from piers. When fish are holding in 20 to 30 feet of water, it's extremely tough to do much to reach them with a cane pole or a fly rod.

The key to casting rods, whether used with a level wind, spinning or spincasting reel, is sensitivity. Today's rods that are made of graphite mixes with other space-age materials can be incredibly sensitive, picking up the most gentle bites and tugs. A really fine rod will register the "feel" of a sinker returning over rocks or mud, and even the gentle pull of a single weed.

The old steel rods were replaced by fiberglass which, in turn,

A mess of panfish is possible even with a plain, old cane pole and plastic bobber. Cane poles continue to be a popular way of vertical presentation for cover-holding panfish.

Panfishing Equipment

was replaced by graphite. Then, companies began combining graphite with fiberglass and other materials to produce rods that were more sensitive, more durable, with high-tensile strength to withstand the continuous flexing of repeated casting. Now, one company, for example, has 26 individually crafted rods which can be used for various species of fish under very specific fishing conditions. These rods range from 100-percent fiberglass to tip-to-butt fiberglass mixed with graphite fibers for long distance casting of light lures. Guides have evolved, too, from ordinary metal to special silicon-carbide, friction-free material.

But, the best isn't always necessary for taking easy-going panfish. When fishing with live bait on a bobber over a honey hole, just about any rig will work. So, it's basically a matter of what you want and can afford. The best and the worst will still fill your stringer, which may be the reason that so many people throughout the country enjoy panfishing.

Cane Poles

In fact, the old cane pole, in its latest versions, is still a favorite among a lot of serious panfishermen. These poles traditionally are made of bamboo in lengths ranging from 12 to 18 feet. Some of the most modern are made now of graphite instead of wood and have nicely wrapped guides. A number are "take-down" models which are easier to transport.

On a real bamboo pole without tied-on guides, the monofilament line is tied to the pole two to three feet from the tip as well as at the tip. Thus, if the tip breaks off, the fish isn't lost, as well. The line is about the same length as the pole so when the pole is raised, the fish is pulled from the water and right into your hands.

A cane pole is particularly effective around submerged trees or brushpiles because the angler can either drop the bait straight down in the openings or put it there with a gentle swing. Also, the fish can be lifted nearly straight up so there's little chance of it being snagged in the twigs and limbs. Sunfish, for example, like to gather in insect-rich lily pad clusters, hyacinth morasses and around weed beds. They'll lie near small openings watching for food, and they're very tough to reach with a standard rod. But, a long pole puts the bait right where you want it without it getting snagged in the surrounding cover. Cane poles are used less often for perch since this panfish is most often found in deeper water.

Even when an angler is working from a boat, an 8- or 10-foot pole with about the same length of line places your bait right next to sunnies seeking shelter in the reeds and lily pads.

Fly Rods

Many fishermen won't use fly rods simply because they're touted as being for experts only—a sophisticated piece of gear used mainly for trout and salmon. Not so.

Actually, a 10-year-old kid with some instruction can learn to use one in a few minutes. After that, it's simply practice. And panfish love fly rods. So do panfishermen. The beauty of a fly rod is that you can cast it easily 30 to 40 feet or more, and the offering will drop onto the water as lightly as thistledown. A rod-cast worm and bobber crashing onto the water's surface can easily spook even the less wary panfish, especially in clear water. And, if the offering lands in an unproductive spot, it can be quickly picked up and cast to a new spot without having to reel in.

Panfish, particularly sunfish, feed heavily on flies. Only with a

fly rod can you cast such tiny, delicate bait. Some of the most excitement a panfisherman can have occurs when he sends a fly or
small popper sailing onto a spawning bed of hungry sunfish.
Strikes often occur right on the surface, and the fight is spectacu-
lar when a half-pound or 1-pound fish goes up against a light,
buggy-whip fly rod. Another advantage is that the rod's flat cast
puts the bait under branches and in spots that spinning and spincasting rigs couldn't touch.

Spincast Reels

Spincast reels are an excellent choice for beginning panfishermen to learn on, and many experts favor them, too. Fairly long
casts can be made even with light lures and baits, and, generally,
there are few tangles.

Spincast reels are closed-face, meaning that the line spool is
enclosed in a cone-shaped cover. Most reels are mounted in the
rod's reel seat on top of the handle, and a push button releases line
when you cast. Other models, however, mount underneath the
rod's handle and line is released with a casting lever which is easily
worked with an index finger. Commonly weighing 6 to 10 ounces,
spincast reels vary in price and quality. While these reels have
drags, unless you're using 1-pound-test line, drags aren't used
much in panfishing. More important when buying a spincast reel
is the gear ratio, often in the 2.5-to-1 to 4-to-1 range. Generally,
the lower ratio offers a slow-speed retrieve, around 10 inches of
line per handle revolution. The higher ratio (4-to-1) brings in
about two feet of line per revolution. Higher ratios give you better
lure control around snags and in current. Also, you can retrieve
your line faster so you can get in more casts. Low ratios, however,
help a panfisherman slow his retrieve during those times when
panfish are reluctant to bite.

Some reels are "semi-closed" for increased casting distance,
and some have a button so that the depth of your lure or bait can
be pre-set. But, no matter the model, the reel needs to match the
rod, and the line needs to match the lure's or bait's weight.

Spinning Reels

The opened-face spinning reel, in small to medium sizes, is
perfect for the light monofilament lines used in panfishing. Spinning reels are often the best bet for making long casts with light

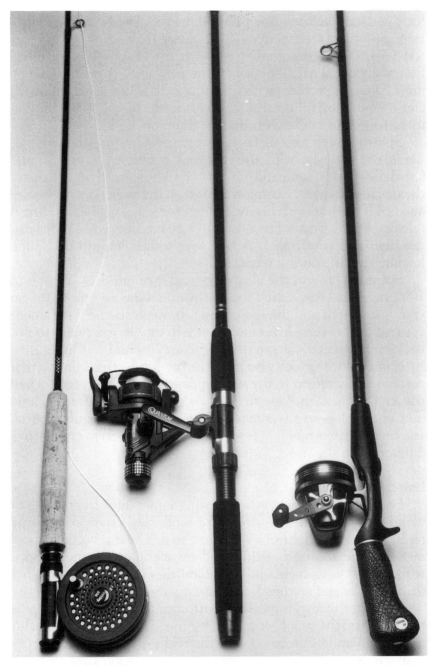

Covering the range of panfish needs are these lightweight rod and reel combinations including (from left) Berkley's fly fishing combo, Zebco's spinning outfit, and Johnson's spincasting rod and reel.

Panfishing Equipment

lures and baits because line peels off the spool with very little friction. Spinning reels generally are faster than spincasting reels, too. Gear ratios, commonly 3.8-to-1 to 6-to-1, provide a retrieval rate of about 20 to 28 inches of line per handle revolution. The most common problem with spinning reels is line tangling which can be cured by filling the reel with fresh, untwisted monofilament to within one-eighth inch of the spool's edge.

Spinning reels also are fairly easy to use. Grasping the rod handle at the reel seat with the reel foot between the middle and fourth fingers (on some rod handles, the whole hand fits in front of the reel foot for a more comfortable grip), the angler opens the bail and holds the line with his index finger. As the cast begins, line is released by the finger. For a smooth lure landing, you can feather the line with your finger. A bail wire rotates around the spool, loading the line during retrieval.

Spinning reels in the ultra-light and medium sizes, about 6 to 10 ounces, are best suited for panfishing. Choose one based on your line weight and the size of the fish. Reels should have a convenient anti-reverse lever and a smooth drag if you prefer to not back-reel, especially if you're using 1- or 2-pound test line.

Some spinning reels also have the pre-set depth setting so that you can easily return to the desired depth. Some reels have a bail trigger for one-hand/one-finger casting, and some feature low-friction spools—an advantage in long casts to wary panfish. And, you can buy spare reel spools for some, enabling you to change to a different line size in seconds.

Baitcasting Reels

Some panfishermen, when casting larger lures to crappies or white bass or when still-fishing for bullheads, prefer baitcasting reels, such as the light units used for bass. These revolving-spool reels provide accurate casting, and are at their best when loaded with at least 8- to 10-pound line. Panfish-size reels often weigh 7 to 10 ounces and feature 3-to-1 to 7-to-1 gear ratios.

To cast, the angler presses a button to free the spool and puts his thumb on the spool (or casting button). To release the lure, lift the thumb and use it to control the reel's speed. Backlash problems can be lessened by adjusting the spool tension knob by holding the rod level and disengaging the spool. Loosen the knob until the lure begins to fall, and then tighten it slightly.

Reels like the Johnson Country Mile (left) and Zebco's Bullet really are hybrids that combine the looks and features of closed-face spincasting reels with opened-face spinning reels.

Pole Reels

Some long poles or rods come fitted with a built-in, simple, single-action reel, and line is fed through the inside of the pole or rod, protecting the line from brush and tangles. The reel may be plastic or metal and is designed to mainly store line. However, some offer drag and anti-reverse features. A more sophisticated pole reel which looks like an automatic fly fishing reel is designed specifically for crappie fishing. The line is pulled out to the desired depth, but when a fish bites, the line is automatically retrieved with the touch of a finger.

Fishing Line

Panfishermen will use lines of various strengths, determined by the approximate number of pounds of pressure required to break the line. While 2- to 6-pound test monofilament line is favored in many panfish situations, some sunfishermen favor 1-pound test or less in open water. However, a few crappie fishermen, tight-lining in thick cover, will use 20- to 40-pound test line to ensure a catch.

Heavy lines are good protection against the inevitable snags, but light lines allow you better feel for the subtle panfish bites. Often, the less visible, lighter lines also result in more strikes from warier panfish, especially in clear water. Light lines can also give more action to lures and live baits, make for longer casts and get you down to the depth where fish are holding more quickly.

Lines are available in varying degrees of stretchability. Fishermen casting for panfish may be better off with line with some stretch; vertical fishermen, with the low-stretch line. Lines with little stretch can help set hooks more effectively and allow the angler to detect bites more readily. Stretchy, flexible lines, though, are easier to cast and don't break as easily when a fish battles the hook. However, line-breaking fish are the exception for most fishermen during panfish outings.

Line also comes in low-visibility colors like clear and green (natural), and high-visibility fluorescent yellow or blue. Anglers seeking wary panfish often favor low-vis, but high-vis lets you see the hits more easily.

Fly-fishing lines include the main fly line, backing line and the leader. Various fly lines which come in floating or sinking versions are used by panfishermen, with level-type lines being inexpensive and suitable for short casts. Double-taper lines—wider in the middle but thinner on the ends—allow a dainty landing of the fly; just what you want for wary panfish. Weight-forward lines are good for long casts, and are useful for casting bulky crappie or white bass streamers or poppers.

Most panfishermen use fly line of size 6 or less (this number should match the number on the fly rod). Lightweight fly lines are for small flies and bugs, and medium lines are for larger panfish tackle. Leaders, connecting the fly line to the lure, can be made from monofilament line or they can be purchased in a ready-made, tapered form.

Terminal Tackle

Hooks, sinkers and bobbers are the basic components of many

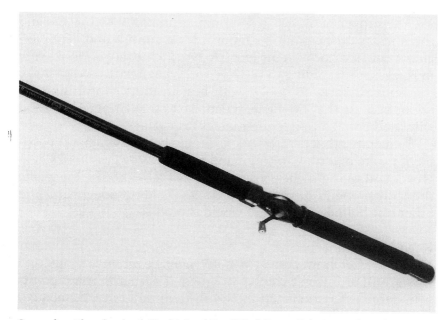

Cane poles with enclosed reels like this South Bend Black Beauty Pole Cat combo make adjusting line length easy and offer protection from snags because the line runs through the pole's center.

panfishing rigs, and should be selected carefully for the species of fish you hope to catch. Unfortunately, many anglers are confused by the seemingly endless variety of sizes and styles available today.

Hooks Are Final Link

Hooks are probably the least expensive item in your tackle box, but they are also the most important. It's the final link and deserves the angler's utmost attention.

Although there are literally thousands of hook designs, three primary considerations govern selection of the proper hook for panfishing. They are size, thickness and shank length.

A hook's size is usually indicated by a number that refers to the distance between the point and the inside of the shank. Hooks increase in size from No. 14 (or even smaller) up through No. 1. As you move from a No. 1 to even larger sizes, the numbering system changes to "aught" designations and hooks increase in size as the number increases. The next largest size after No. 1 is 1/0 (one-aught), and larger hooks are numbered 2/0, 3/0, 4/0 and so on. The 2/0 size is the largest hook most anglers who fish for panfish would ever use, and then only to fish for large crappies.

The proper hook size is determined primarily by the size and the fragility of the panfish's mouth. Most sunfish and perch anglers would use hooks in the No. 6 to No. 10 size range. Hooks vary in thickness, according to the size and type of wire used to make the hook. Light-wire hooks work best in most panfishing situations because they do the least damage to small, fragile baits and will bend enough to free themselves from snags.

Remember that barbless hooks should be used whenever possible if you're planning to catch and release. Weedless hooks help prevent snagging in heavy vegetation. Treble hooks, especially the spring-wound models, are best for holding doughbaits and other soft bullhead baits that would slip off single hooks.

Keep Hooks Sharp

No matter how perfect a hook may be in size, shape and strength, it still won't catch fish unless it is sharp! Sharp points penetrate better and catch more fish than dull ones. Remember that even new hooks may need to be sharpened, and check your hooks to be sure they have sharp points each time you bait them.

Choosing The Right Sinker

Even the most sophisticated panfish angler must at one time or another resort to fishing with sinkers if he wants to catch fish. Sinkers of one form or another are a necessary element for trolling, bottomfishing in current and other panfishing tactics.

Sinkers are simply weights made of lead or other metal. They are molded in many different shapes and sizes, but all serve primarily to carry bait or lures down to a particular depth where fish are feeding. Choice depends mostly on the type of fish being sought, the depth to be fished, type of bottom and other factors such as current and wave action.

Loosely divided, sinkers fit into two categories: attached or fixed sinkers and sliding or slip sinkers. Each has its advantages. When selecting fixed sinkers, always use the lightest that will still carry your bait to the desired depth. Split shot, clinch sinkers, rubber-core sinkers, bell sinkers, bank sinkers, pyramid sinkers, trolling and walking sinkers all fit within this category.

Most split shots are small, round weights which pinch directly onto the line. Their small and varied sizes make them ideal for balancing lightweight bobber rigs. Some have small "ears" for easier

A sampling of good hooks for panfish fishing include hookmaker VMC's prepacked assortment (top), VMC's O'Shaughnessy trebles shown in No. 14 and No. 20 (center left), VMC's Aberdeen in No. 2/0 and No. 16 (center right) and VMC's baitholder hooks (bottom) in sizes ranging from No. 2/0 through No. 12. Popular panfish sizes are No. 6 and No. 8.

Panfishing Equipment

removal, but these also pick up weeds more easily. Split shot sizes range from tiny "dust" shot (sizes 12 to 8) up through sizes 7 to 1, BB, AA and SSG (swan shot). Sizes 8 to 3 are among those most commonly used for panfish. Shot are usually attached far enough above the hook so they don't interfere with the bait's natural action. Crunching shot on with pliers or repositioning the shot on the line without first opening the split can damage your line.

Clinch sinkers, so named because they "clinch" the line and do not require threading and thus retying the hook, are like elongated split shot and are sometimes used when an angler needs more weight than a split shot provides. They are designed for still fishing rather than trolling because they tend to twist the line as they're pulled through the water. Rubber-core sinkers are similar to clinch sinkers in both form and function, but have a rubber strip through the split which holds the sinker in place. The rubber insert makes it easy to attach or detach the sinker from the line with bait attached.

Bell sinkers, also known as dipsey or bass-casting sinkers, are molded around a brass swivel which prevents line twist when used in drift fishing or when bouncing a bait on the bottom. Bank sinkers are six-sided and molded entirely of lead, including the eye. They cast well and are a good substitute for the bell sinker because they are less apt to cause line twisting. Pyramid sinkers, as the name suggests, are molded in the shape of a pyramid, with a brass wire eye on the square end. They're especially good for holding bottom in strong currents or when there is heavy wave action on the surface.

Trolling or bead-chain sinkers are overlooked by many panfishermen, but they are extremely useful when trolling or drifting for crappies, perch and other panfish. They come in keeled or torpedo-shaped models, and planing versions have wings that cause the sinker to dive, achieving more depth. The use of beaded swivels can prevent line twist. Walking sinkers are becoming more popular as a means of avoiding bottom snags. They're made with a piece of heavy wire that is bent at a right angle with a swivel attached to one arm and a weight on the other arm. This design permits the sinker to walk across the bottom without snagging. Their relatively high price discourages many anglers from using them, but they quickly pay for themselves in situations where most weights would be snagged and lost.

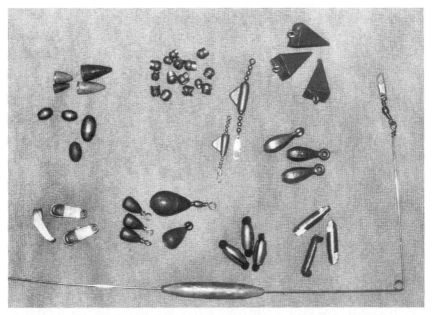

Common types of sinkers are (clockwise from top left) the bullet, split shot, keeled trolling, pyramid, bank, clinch, rubber-core, bell, walking slip, egg and (below) walking sinker.

Sliding or slip sinkers let the fish swim off without feeling any resistance as the weight resting on the bottom lets the line slip through. A barrel swivel or a split shot is sometimes used below the sinker to keep it from sliding too close to the hook.

Three common examples of sliding sinkers are the egg, bullet and walking slip sinker. Egg or barrel sinkers have a hole through the middle so the line slides freely. They are available in many sizes that are useful for panfishing and are a common component of many stationary live-bait rigs. Bullet sinkers are similar but are cone-shaped to provide minimal drag and relative weedlessness. Walking slip sinkers have a flattened "foot" shape and are used with a stopper when casting or trolling bait along the bottom.

Multi-Purpose Bobbers

Whether you call them bobbers, floats or corks, these simple devices perform several functions which are important to panfish anglers. In addition to suspending the bait at the right depth and providing a visual cue that a fish has taken the bait, they also add weight so you can cast those tiny, $1/16$-, $1/32$- and even $1/64$-ounce lures accurately and the proper distance. They keep the bait moving efficiently in the panfish "strike" zones, and keep the bait suspended above potential snags.

Balanced with the proper weight, bobbers can be amazingly sensitive to the panfish's light bites. With the use of a bobber, live or artificial bait can be presented in a "normal" way that won't spook wary panfish. Bobbers also let you know how close you're fishing to the bottom or cover, a function that is especially important when fishing for redear sunfish and other bottom feeders. For example, if you want your bait just inches off the bottom, you raise your bobber until it no longer sits upright in the water. When the bobber sits at an angle, you can lower it the distance that you want to fish off the bottom and return the bait to that position.

There are several styles of bobbers, and, naturally, each has its strong points. Most are made from hard plastic, foam, wood, cork or porcupine quills. They may be round, pear-shaped, cigar-shaped, pencil-shaped or a combination of these shapes. When selecting a bobber, take into account the size of the bait, the depth of the fish and how visible the float is to you and the fish. Round bobbers, for example, may provide too much resistance if the bait is taken by a small panfish, and it may result in the fish dropping the bait before it is hooked.

The two basic types of bobbers are the fixed which attach firmly to the line with a spring-loaded hook, peg, rubber band or other such device, and the sliding or slip bobbers that move freely along the line.

Fixed bobbers are best suited for fishing waters no deeper than the length of your rod or pole. This style of float allows the bait to remain at a preset depth during your retrieve. In deeper water, use a slip bobber to cut down on casting problems. With a sliding bobber, the entire rigging (bobber, sinker and hook) can be reeled almost up to the rod tip. A rubber band or small bobber stop placed on the line at the proper depth will keep the bait in the desired target zone.

The familiar round, red-over-white snap-on bobbers are most frequently used by panfish anglers because they're convenient to use and easily seen. However, they do provide the greatest resistance. Tiny, cigar-shaped floats made of foam or cork offer very little resistance, and are also very popular among serious panfishermen. They are held in place at the desired depth with a small wooden or plastic peg.

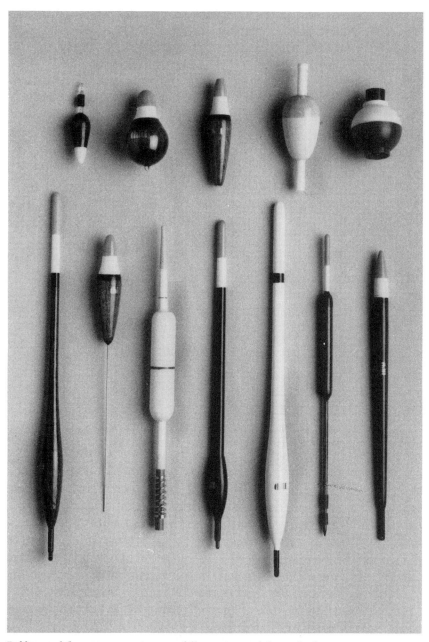

Bobbers and floats now come in many different sizes and shapes for fine-tuning presentations under various conditions. From left, top row, are three Thill Tackle Co. floats, the Mini Stealth, Stream 'n Brook Master and the Center Slider, and the more often seen conventional oval and round plastic bobbers. The bottom row shows Thill's TG Waggler, TG Waggler in white, the Shy Bite and Smooth Stream, all of which are streamlined pencil floats.

Panfishing Equipment

Slender pencil-style floats are a good choice for panfish such as this crappie. This style provides very little resistance when a fish takes the bait.

Pencil bobbers have been around a long time, and are another favorite of panfishermen. The pencil shape also offers little resistance so it's not easily detected by panfish. And, long, thin "quill" bobbers are excellent for panfishing in calm, shallow water because they're extremely sensitive to the slightest nibble and enter the water with only a tiny splash. While these lightweight bobbers may be difficult to use in windy conditions, casting bobbers, or bubbles, are designed to add extra distance to your casts in the wind. Casting bubbles can be partially filled with water to provide added weight for easier casting.

Among the newest bobber innovations on the American market are lighted bobbers and European-style bobbers. Lighted bobbers have a small, battery-powered light on top, allowing the angler to detect bites even on the darkest night. The European-style

Complete Angler's Library

bobbers which tend to be quite small are some of the most sensitive ever devised, making them a potent addition to the panfisherman's arsenal. However, they may be difficult to find in many areas of the country.

Sonar

Electronic sonar instruments help panfishermen find ideal fishing depths, structure, bottom types and cover—and the fish themselves, especially species that frequently suspend such as crappies and white bass but also bluegills, perch and others. Sonar (Sound Navigation Ranging) also alerts you to dangerously shallow water when boating, and can be used while dock fishing and ice fishing. (Use of sonar units for fishing is discussed in greater detail in chapter 18.)

A flasher sonar unit probably is the best all-round buy for panfishermen because it gives an immediate picture of the bottom and panfish depth.

Flashers

Several types of sonar units are available, but flasher-type units are probably best suited for the panfisherman. Flashers are reliable, and they're compact and easy to transport—perfect companions for small boats. They're also economical, often priced at less than a hundred dollars. Despite the relatively low cost, flashers can give you all the structure, cover and fish location information you really need. And, flashers show what's below you immediately, helpful not only in fishing situations but in safe navigation. On other units the picture is slightly delayed.

Flashers, featuring a clock-like dial marked with depth in feet, show a constant mark of light at the depth of the bottom and at zero feet. When you pass over fish, trees, or other objects, the unit flashes in between the two constant points, at the object's depth. Flashers don't "detail" the objects like other units; however, with a little practice, you can distinguish features such as the bottom, fish, trees and other structure.

The Flasher's Transducer

In flashers (as in all sonar units) a transducer is attached via a cable to the main unit. The transducer, placed in the water, emits signals. The signals hit bottom (or fish) and bounce back to the transducer and the depths are marked on the sonar's screen. By fishing directly over the transducer, you can see both the marks of the fish and of your descending lure or bait.

Transducers are made in different types, some more suited for panfishing than others. Mainly, the different types cover different amounts of water. Some transducers cover wide angles (about 20 degrees) and are great for shallow panfishing. Slightly narrower angles or "cones" (about 15 degrees) are good for deeper water panfishing. Cones of 10 degrees or less aren't as practical; they're more for deep-sea water.

Sonar units are also available with different depth ranges. If you strictly panfish, there's no need to spend extra money on units which read over 100 feet.

Get The Most Out Of The Flasher

Anglers should thoroughly read the owner's manual to learn how to properly install the flasher and set the dials. For panfishing, it is important to keep the unit's sensitivity turned up to the right

Looking For Suspended Schools

An effective way of locating suspended sunfish is by attaching a transducer on a movable bracket to the stem of your trolling motor so that the transducer can be set at an angle (as shown) so that you don't have to run over them in order to find them.

level. Otherwise, the fish won't show up. Properly set, the flasher should register two or more bottoms instead of one. Just disregard the echoed bottoms.

If you know the fish you seek often swim within a few feet of the surface, one trick is to mount the transducer on the trolling motor bottom in such a way that the transducer can be swiveled 90 degrees (so it points straight out to open water instead of to the bottom.) Then, by turning the direction of the trolling motor, you can find fish just under the surface out away from the boat. You'll not only know which direction the fish are (the direction the transducer faces) but also the number of feet to make your cast.

Portable boxes containing the flasher unit have been available for certain flasher models. These are great choices for anglers who frequently travel and rent boats. You can also easily make a port-

Sonar can help you find panfish that are suspended or located around structure far from shore. A factory installed liquid crystal display unit ensures proper transducer placement.

Complete Angler's Library

able rig; build an open-top, three-sided box from quarter-inch ply-wood (or sheet metal) just large enough to house the flasher and a power source, such as two 6-volt lantern batteries or a 12-volt mo-torcycle battery. (You might even have enough space for your day's fishing lures.) Bolt the unit to the bottom or sides so you can view the flasher's dial through the open side. A short dowel or rope, threaded through holes in the box's side, serves as a handle. These units, and some made commercially, are ideal for ice fishing as well as open water fishing.

Other Sonar Units

Liquid crystal units (LCDs and LCGs) and video units are good fish finders and come with many selectable features, but they generally cost a bit more than flashers. Paper graph units pick up great detail, though they are considerably costlier than flashers, they consume more battery power, and the graph paper occasion-ally needs replacing. When it comes to panfishing, a paper graph may be best suited for crappie-tournament anglers. Some com-petitive anglers employ two different types of sonar, installing one at each end of the boat.

Digital depth units give a numerical depth reading and are mainly used for navigation. Small, hand-held sonar units show depth via a pointer on a dial, and are mainly useful in showing depth and depth changes. Other electronic devices show pH, oxy-gen, lure color selection, or temperature, which may clue you in on where fish might or might not be. However, a sonar unit, in-cluding a simple flasher unit, can tell you the same thing, only so-nar can't tell you the reason why fish are or aren't present.

3

Baits And Lures

Worms or minnows? Jigs or spinners? What should you pack to take along to your favorite panfish hole? Live baits and artificial lures each account for panfish galore and each offer advantages. Many panfishermen swear by live baits year-round. The baits not only appeal to the fish's sense of sight and hearing, but also to the senses of taste and smell.

Using artificials may consume less fishing time; however, baits may be the only items the panfish may be interested in, particularly during cold spells or when the water is muddy. Also, panfish generally hold onto baits longer, giving the angler a better chance for a hookup.

Minnows

Minnows are a great bait for crappies, perch and white bass, and they're an overlooked bait for jumbo sunfish. Minnows also help you nab bullheads, white perch and yellow bass.

Live minnows are legal to use in most states. (Of course, check the state regulations before gathering and using any live bait.) Minnows up to 4 inches or so have captured lunker crappies and white bass; however, these and other panfish are more normally taken on 1 1/2 to 2-inch baits. Tiny minnows are tops when the fish aren't feeding heavily, and, at all times, for bluegills.

The "crappie minnows" that are available at baitshops generally can be almost any small forage fish. Fathead minnows (called

Longears like this one taken on a cricket bait feed primarily on insects and small fish. Obviously, crickets and minnows are good choices when you're out looking for longear "holes."

Baits And Lures

tuffies in some regions) are tough, long-lasting baits. Small shiners, though more fragile, are also popular. Other panfish takers include small alewives, darters, dace and chubs. In the South, small threadfin shad often take large crappies and white bass.

Baitfish can be bought in most areas, but sometimes shops run out. Anyway, minnows caught in the same lake being fished often work best. Gathering some species such as threadfin shad calls for more sophisticated techniques, but many shallower-water minnows can be easily gathered with a seine or trap. Clear plastic traps are good for streams, while wire traps work well in lakes. Simply look for minnows and set out a trap baited with oatmeal, cornmeal, bread or cracker crumbs. Check it after several hours.

Or, place a lift net on bottom, throw bait over it and lift it out of water when the minnows arrive. Minnows such as fatheads are also seined with long nets by pairs of anglers working along weedy shores or in streams.

The livelier the minnows, the more strikes you generally get. Keeping them lively during the summer may involve investing in a small battery-run aerator for the minnow bucket or keep the minnows in your boat's livewell. Another option is to use an insulated foam minnow bucket and put several ice cubes in the water to lower the water temperature and decrease the minnows' oxygen use. Avoiding overcrowding the bucket and keeping it out of the sun also helps.

The rest of the year, metal or plastic buckets should work satisfactorily. The perforated inner buckets, or one-piece buckets which are perforated at the top can be placed over the boat's side.

Earthworms

Garden worms and nightcrawlers or nightcrawler pieces rank as one of the most important and universal panfish baits. Soft and action-packed, they often work great for sunfish, perch, bullheads and other catfish. Worms also catch crappies, rock bass, white perch and other panfish. Nightcrawlers are usually too large to fish whole on most panfish-sized hooks, but a small piece may produce as well as other baits.

When you can't find worms at the baitshop, which is a rarity, worms can be found in gardens, compost piles or other moist fertile soil. Nightcrawlers can be harvested at night on grassy areas, especially after rains. Bring a can and a flashlight, and dip your fin-

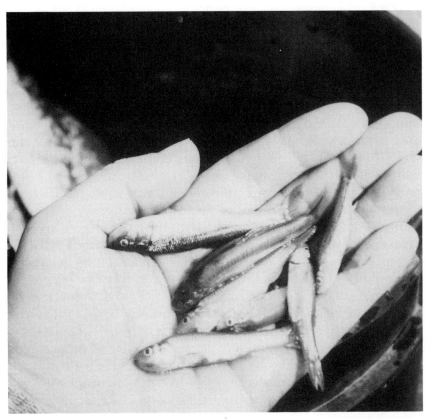

Fresh, lively minnows such as this group are a big plus when you're going after panfish. Care should be taken to keep them that way when you get to your favorite fishing spot.

gers in sawdust to keep worms from slipping back into their holes as you pull gently.

Commercial worm bedding feeds and worm boxes are available to keep worms for extended periods of time. Fresh and lively worms catch the most fish. To keep worms the most active they should be stored at not more than 60 degrees.

Ice in a plastic bag placed in the bait box will make for livelier bait and heavier panfish catches in warm weather. A portable homemade container to carry while fishing can be fashioned from a metal can. Cut out both ends and cover with clear plastic lids.

Larval Baits

Insects are one of the prime panfish forages. Small larvae (grub) baits are excellent for sunfish and other panfish year-round, and they may be *the* bait to use in colder water. Larvae also add extra appeal to artificials, and they make great chum, wherever chumming is legal.

Larvae include mealworms, waxworms, goldenrod grubs, caddisworms and mousies. Other aquatic insect baits include hellgrammites, stone fly and mayfly nymphs (wigglers). Hellgrammites (immature dobsonflies), often a couple inches long or more, are good for catching perch, rock bass, catfish and other fish. Baits such as maggots (bottle fly larvae) are commercially available in various colors. Many fresh larvae are available only in wintertime at bait shops, but preserved grubs generally are available anytime.

Immature aquatic insects can be captured in small streams by using a window screen held to the bottom at a 45-degree angle. It takes the help of another person who moves rocks upstream of the screen, pushing larvae toward it. Other larvae can be dug out of shore mud and muck. Caddisworms, found in tiny cases of sand or plant matter, can easily be handpicked or netted. Aquatic creatures can be kept for short periods in a minnow bucket filled with adequate vegetation.

Gallworms can be cut out of goldenrod galls and other weeds. Various fish-enticing grubs are found under old tree bark or in rotting stumps. Mealworms commonly live in old cornmeal. Wasp larvae, harvestable when adults are dormant, make excellent panfish chow.

Crickets, Grasshoppers And Other Insects

Crickets rate as top-notch summertime baits for sunfish, and some bait shops offer them year-round. Occasionally, you also catch crappies, perch and white bass on them. Crickets can be raised at home, or can be captured under stones, boards or in basements. Crickets (as well as grasshoppers and katydids, other good panfish catchers) can be also caught with homemade nets in grassy fields and cropland.

While fishing, you can keep these insects in a narrow-necked bottle, covered with a perforated cap. Only one at a time will move through the bottleneck. Or use regular wire cricket/grasshopper cages, available in tackle shops and from catalogs.

Catalpa worms—black and white caterpillars found on catalpa trees—can work wonders on sunfish. Tent caterpillars can be easily gathered by just removing the whole web. Adult mayflies and

Live larvae baits are always popular with aggressive sunfish. These baits—(clockwise from upper left) mousies, Euro larvae, waxworms and grubs—are effective under most conditions and are good choices when panfish are being particularly choosy.

Baits And Lures

similar flies are great baits for sunfish, crappies and others. After living on a lake or stream bottom, they hatch and rise to the surface. The flies can be caught by hand or with a net, especially at night with lights.

Leeches
These aquatic worms work well for sunfish, crappies and perch. Leeches don't come off a hook easily, and they make lots of enticing movements. Northern baitshops often carry leeches, though they're found in the wild in other regions, too. To catch them, submerge a burlap sack of meat scraps overnight in the shallows. Usually, you will find leeches on, or inside, the sack come morning. Be sure to use ribbon or tiger leeches, not the softer bodied horse or medicine leech which fish seem to avoid.

Crayfish
Tiny crayfish, about 1 $\frac{1}{2}$ inches long, catch crappies, perch, rock bass and bullheads. Small "softshell" crayfish, ones which have just molted, are particularly effective. Crayfish tails, peeled or unpeeled, entice these same species, and crayfish meat also is a hot bait for sunfish, especially redears.

You may not find tiny crayfish in baitshops, but you might catch them around rocks near shore. (Check your state's regulations first.) At night, you might check the shallows with a flashlight, and capture them by hand or with a fish-meat baited hook. Or place a dipnet on the bottom and lead crayfish to it with either a meat bait or by coaxing it with a stick. Also, crayfish traps can be set and baited with fish or meat.

Store crayfish in a large minnow bucket or foam box with water and weeds on the bottom. Change the water now and then to keep it fresh and to keep the crayfish cool. A bag of ice in the box helps in hot weather.

Shrimp
A relative of the crayfish is the freshwater grass shrimp, a bait worth trying for sunfish, crappies, perch and rock bass. Shrimp, also called scuds, grow two inches or more. They're available at some baitshops in the extreme southwestern U.S., or you can try netting them in weedy water. Shrimp can be stored in a bucket or cooler box and can be kept lively with a live-bait aerator. Pieces of

Preserved baits manufactured by Uncle Josh bait company specifically for panfish fishing include (left to right) pork rind, grass shrimp, maggots and crickets.

frozen shrimp, available at grocery stores, also make an effective panfish bait.

Frogs

Tiny frogs may be the most overlooked bait for big bluegills. They also entice bullheads and, at times, yellow perch.

Frogs can be captured by hand or with a net along riverbanks or lakeshores, and can be kept in a commercially-made frog box or in a foam cooler containing air holes, a little water and a board or weeds. Frogs need to be kept cool.

Fish And Clam Meat

All minnow-eating panfish may eat cut fish. At least, it's an option when you run out of other baits. A small strip cut from fresh fish belly may catch sunfish, crappies, perch and others when tipped on a hook or artificial. Fish eyes, fins and eggs also nab many panfish. Meat from clams and mussels catches sunfish, especially redears.

Preserved Or Dead Baits
Tiny preserved or fresh but dead minnows catch sunfish, crappies, white bass and perch. They're good, too, bottomfished for bullheads. Other preserved baits available include freeze-dried baits (which must be soaked in water) such as maggots, crickets, grass shrimp, crayfish, earthworms and grubs. When drifted in streams or wavy water or when retrieved, many of these look quite life-like.

Pork Rind
Tiny pork rinds, with a soft baitfish texture, appear life-like and tasty to sunfish, crappies, perch and others. They're available in various colors and in straight strips, v-shape and other styles as small as a half inch. Panfish-size pieces can also be cut from larger pork rinds.

Artificial/Natural Baits
Combination artificial/natural baits are being developed for panfishermen. Some consisting of natural protein are combined with artificial material, and aren't perishable like living baits so they can be tackle-box stored. Some resemble forage-like grubs and leeches, and they come in a variety of different colors and fish-attracting scents.

Other scent products come in putty form and can be molded onto hooks. They leave an odor trail in the water. Also, special bottled fish attractants have been developed strictly for panfish. Scent can be added to live baits or artificials to make them more appealing. Of course, other scent baits such as stinkbaits have long been available for bullhead and catfishermen.

Live baits sometimes out-fish artificial lures by a wide margin. Sometimes, however, it's the other way around, and more anglers are employing artificial lures than ever before. If you don't lose many to snags, artificials can be less expensive than minnows or other bait. And, lures allow for quicker fishing. Sometimes, the fish are gone by the time you catch a bait in your bait container

Small crayfish-imitation crankbaits such as this Rebel Deep Teeny Wee–Crawfish can be an excellent enticement for rock bass, just as good often times as the real, live bait.

Baits And Lures

and then wrestle with it to hook it. An artificial can usually be re-cast immediately.

Jigs

Jigs are by far the most popular artificial for taking panfish. These lures imitate the size and shape of minnows or small insects, or they might just appear to be generic food, still attractive to opportunistic panfish. Jigs can also be fished with a variety of retrieves to match forage movements.

A typical, effective panfish jig may have a plastic or marabou body, weighing about $1/16$ or $1/32$ ounce, in one of a number of colors, and might always catch a few fish. However, dozens of styles are available today, and in a particular situation, another jig might attract 10 times as many fish.

The best jig choice (and this applies to other artificials, too) depends on panfish size, their current diet and sky and water conditions. To be prepared for any situation, your tackle box should house several jig styles, colors and weights.

Most sunfish jigs range from $1/100$ ounce to $1/16$ ounce. (Feather-weight ice fishing jigs work well in warm months, too.) The weight needs to be matched with the monofilament. If underwater snags and the fish's wariness call for about 4-pound line, a $1/64$-ounce jig may give a good and necessary slow speed during casting and retrieving, unless the bluegills are deep. Then, a heavier lure would be better.

Perch jigs and crappie jigs range from around $1/100$ to $1/8$ ounce, occasionally up to $1/4$ ounce.

Most panfish jigs have ball-shaped lead heads which work fine in open water. A jighead with a broad, flat face, however, can reduce snagging when used in woody cover. Pulled over a limb, this jighook usually remains in a upward position, away from the wood. Also, some narrow-shaped heads may result in fewer snags that occur in rocks.

While a marabou-bodied jig may be a killer one day, a plastic jig may catch the most another day from that same panfish group. Each material has advantages.

Plastic offers the softness of a real grub or minnow, and these jigs allow you to change jig color quicker by just slipping on a new body. A quick change can get you more fish from a school when action seems to be slowing down.

Plastic jigs consist of curly-tailed, tube (with multi-strand tails) and straight-tailed. Some straight-tailed jigs have a widened tail which, as it sinks or is retrieved, creates a wiggling movement panfish often can't resist. Another straight-bodied style has plastic side "wings" which glide very slowly through the water, often tempting bluegills, crappies and perch. Each style has a different action, and the best one for the day can only be discovered through test fishing.

Marabou, noted for life-like movements even when the jigs are virtually still, works for many panfish presentations. One advantage of marabou is that it holds more attractor scent than many plastic jigs which can result in more fish. (Some scent brands cake up the marabou and kill the action, so be sure to check this possibility before use.)

Bucktail or hair jigs also hold lots of scent; however, their motion is more subtle than the marabou's. But that's a possible advantage if the panfish require a subdued presentation.

Some jigs are available with bodies built with various bulky materials. A jig with lots of bucktail is an example. Bulky jigs, possibly with a dash of shiny mylar, are good choices for super-slow fishing for big panfish in murky water. Scantily dressed jigs—with maybe just a few mylar strands—are possible choices for fishing in clear water.

Panfish are caught on jigs ranging from a half-inch to more than 3 inches. Jigs about 1 inch are usually tops for bluegills and 1 to 2 inches for crappies and perch. As a rule, decrease the length for clear water under a bright sky and increase the size when fishing under darker conditions. Also, dissecting a panfish you've caught can give helpful clues to ideal length. Even trophy-size panfish may be chowing down tiny items for some reason and it may help to match that size. Jig tails can be clipped off or, to increase size, tipped with a plastic tail or natural bait.

Jig Sizes And Styles

Different brands of jigs, even those of the same length and weight, come with varying hook sizes. Fish-hooking problems can often be overcome by choosing jigs with the right-sized hook. The tiniest jig hooks (around No. 10) are usually best for most sunfish species. Crappies are taken on hooks ranging from tiny to rather large, but beware of certain in-between-sized hooks which frequently hit the thin membrane between the lips and the roof of the mouth because they tend to tear in this area. So watch how the panfish you do boat are hooked, and then change hook sizes or styles if necessary. A honing stone should be kept in the tackle box to give hook points a triangular sharpening whenever needed.

Because many panfish lurk around cover, jig hooks which can be easily bent and freed when snagged are an asset. Some panfish experts heat the shank's bend with a match. This weakens the hook enough so it bends easily when snagged on wood or rocks yet still holds the largest panfish.

A few panfish jigs are available in snag-proof styles, such as those with hook guards or plastic bodies which cover the hook point. These jigs may mean fewer hooked panfish; however, they're an option to think about.

Panfish inhabiting clear water are commonly fooled with tiny jigs in subdued colors like olive, medium brown and gray, as well as brighter colors like chartreuse. In dingier water, the subdued colors are harder to see so slightly larger lures in bright colors like chartreuse and pearl white are best. Tests show solid colors can be more visible than multi colors.

Bluegills will hit a variety of colors—white, brown, black, yellow and so on. Perch often love bright colors—yellow, red and white. Crappies? In tests, chartreuse beat other colors by a small margin, even on a super-clear reservoir.

NAFC members always catch more panfish, though, by having several colors ready. One color might match the forage being eaten, but even after several panfish have hit that color, trying any other color usually results in extra fish.

Spinnerbaits

Many panfish are caught on spinnerbaits, either single-spin baits with the spinner on a wire arm or jigs with a tail spinner or under-the-body spinner. Spinnerbaits should be small although some lunker crappies are taken on bass-size spinnerbaits. An advantage of wire-armed models is that in woody-cover water they're fairly snag-proof, and, in murky water, the brightness and the vibrations attract fish. They work best in shallow water, and they must be fished quite slowly. A Colorado-style blade accommodates that best.

Wire-armed spinnerbaits are relatively snagless and suited for

This easily carried array of poppers, jigs and artificials was more than enough to take some nice panfish on a fly rod. Using lightweight tackle adds excitement to the catch.

panfish lurking in lily pads or other thick weeds even when the water is clear. Plain jigs may hook a higher percentage of fish, but with spinnerbaits, you aren't always pulling and re-bending hooks. Jigs with spinners on the tail or under the body, of course, aren't as snag-proof, but they're good choices for murky or dark water. They are also great for long-distance casting to white bass.

Panfish Spinners

Small spinners are fun lures for shallow-water bluegills, as well as excellent fan-casting lures for roving crappies or white bass swimming just beneath the surface. Spinner/flies, weight-forward, and other spinners, with or without tipped bait, also account for many perch.

While spinners offer an attention-getting flash, small, plain

jigs might work better if the fish aren't active. Some fishermen replace the spinner's treble hook with a single hook so fish can be
unhooked quickly. The same considerations in choosing color
and size should be made as in selecting jigs.

Tiny Spoons And Crankbaits

Inch-long spoons can capture bluegills, and 1 to 2-inch spoons
are appropriate for perch and crappies. However, some Southern
anglers tie on silver, hammered jigging spoons which may measure
up to about 3 inches for taking big crappies. Small wobblers or
other thin-metal spoons can be trolled or cast and retrieved slowly
for shallow fish. Heavier spoons, including the hammered jigging
spoons, are best for deep, vertical jigging for perch and crappies.

Today, many crankbaits in small, panfish sizes are being produced, and some crappie trollers now use crankbaits exclusively.
Crankbaits around $1/4$ ounce and 2 inches or smaller are best for
crappies, perch and rock bass. White bass often hit larger
crankbaits. Besides being good trolling lures, floating and diving
crankbaits can be ideal for casting and retrieving to shallow panfish. Tiny topwater plugs which allow a slow retrieve are top
choices for surface-feeding panfish.

Fly Fishing Lures

Bluegills commonly hit tiny poppers, rubber spiders and various dry and wet flies, and provide great battles for fly fishermen.
Wet and dry flies, bucktails, streamers and small poppers can all
catch crappies. Perch, when fairly shallow, are taken with a variety of flies, too.

Dry flies and tiny poppers are appropriate for any surfacing-
panfish situation. Wet flies and nymphs are a good choice in
springtime when panfish commonly eat the tiny aquatic insects
these lures represent. Baitfish imitations like streamers and bucktails may be most appropriate overall for crappies, and big bluegills
and perch hit them, too. All flies work best when the fish are shallow or near the surface, because panfish strikes in deep water are
often too difficult to detect on fly line.

Tackle Boxes

Today's panfishermen enjoy the most convenient tackle boxes
and lure containers ever built. Fortunately, panfishermen can get

by with small, easy-to-carry containers because the lures and tackle are so small.

Soft nylon tote bags are popular. Their clear, tough soft-plastic compartments feature easy viewing for selection.

Wade or bank fishermen now can mount a small tackle box on the front of their belts. Yet another container consists of individual round, hard plastic compartments which can be screwed together. Of course, rigid plastic tackle boxes, in many designs including some specially made up for panfishing, still reign. They're great if you want to carry pliers, scent bottles and other large equipment items.

One new design is a main box full of small individual plastic lure (or bait) containers, allowing the angler to store and select the container needed for that day's fishing from the master box.

4

The Ultimate Panfish Boat

Considering the extensive variety of boats and boating equipment available on today's market, it would be ludicrous to pretend one could design a panfishing boat that would fulfill every angler's needs and fancies. Nevertheless, many panfishermen considering the purchase of their first boat want advice for selecting a craft rigged especially for this style of fishing.

To help in that respect, we've dreamed up the ultimate panfish boat. It certainly won't meet every angler's expectations, but it's one of the best options available when considering versatility, comfort, safety and economy. If you want a quality craft suitable for most panfishing situations, this is one option you should strongly consider.

The Boat

Before purchasing a panfishing boat, you should ask yourself some questions. Among the most important are 1) Does the craft offer the safety and stability required for the waters I fish? 2) Can I use it when fishing timber-infested lakes, rock-strewn streams, shallow waters and other panfish haunts where I must navigate over or through obstacles of cover or structure? 3) Will it safely accommodate all the fishing equipment and boating accessories I want to use? 4) Is it lightweight and compact enough for easy transport and launching on the waters I fish? 5) Does the craft meet my standards for durability and comfort? 6) Is it versatile

A boat for panfish doesn't have to be expensive. It should be deep enough to be safe on choppy water and have enough power to reach distant spots. Running lights allow fishing at night.

The Ultimate Panfish Boat

enough to use on a variety of panfishing waters? 7) Can I afford it?

By answering these questions, most panfishermen will be able to quickly eliminate several styles of boats. For instance, big bass boats cost too much to make them a feasible choice for most anglers. On top of that, they are too big to launch on many of the out-of-the-way panfish waters where modern boat ramps are an unavailable luxury.

One- or two-man mini bass boats limit the amount of gear you can carry and shouldn't be used in waters with high waves or strong current, or where anglers must cover long distances. Large semi-v hulls are suitable for most open-water situations, but they're difficult to comfortably maneuver in shallow or heavily timbered waters. Canoes are great for stream fishing, but they don't offer much in the way of stability and speed. Anglers can't move around much to cast or fight a fish. And though square-sterned models can accommodate outboard motors, horsepower must, for safety reasons, be limited.

Ask the same seven questions about a small semi-v hull or johnboat, and the answers are likely to be yes in all cases. That's why this kind of craft is our selection for the ultimate panfish boat.

We want our boat to be safe under all conditions that panfishermen might normally encounter, and stable enough to allow the angler to move around when fishing. Because these boats have a shallow draft, especially johnboats, they're perfect for navigating shallow, cover-infested waters where panfish are often found. We need plenty of room for all the gear most panfishermen use, and the boat should rate high in durability, comfort and ease of being transported.

Our panfish boat can be rowed, paddled, poled or driven with a motor, and unlike other types of boats, has a seat affixed close to the water on the boat's bow that permits the angler to scull the craft with a small paddle. Best of all, these boats are relatively inexpensive, making them an excellent choice for anglers with a limited budget.

Of course, there are a variety of options to consider when selecting a panfish boat. One is construction. For our ultimate panfish boat, we'll select aluminum, because it's more durable than fiberglass and most other boat materials. Run a fiberglass or plastic boat up on a stump, and you'll be bailing water. A medium- to heavy-gauge aluminum boat will be able to better withstand this

Mini bass boats like this two-seater are popular with may panfish anglers because they're light-weight and easily carried. However, they're easily swamped and have limited space for gear.

kind of unintentional physical abuse.

A square-bowed johnboat is okay, but boats with a semi-v bow cut through waves better, thus giving a smoother, safer ride on choppy waters. There's little cost difference in the two kinds of construction, so we'll invest in a semi-v craft.

Size is another option. Many panfish waters don't have modern launching facilities, so we may often have to carry our boat some distance to the water. Therefore, we want a boat that is relatively lightweight. Still, we don't want a boat that's too small, because we have lots of gear to carry along, and we want a safe, stable vessel. Considering these factors, we'll make our ultimate panfish boat a mid-sized model, 12 to 14 feet long and ideally less than 48 inches wide. That's safe for most waters, roomy enough for all our equipment, but not so big that it becomes unwieldy. This size can

The Ultimate Panfish Boat

be carried in the back of a pickup, too.

We should also consider the deck layout. Since we'll be carrying friends and family along on some of our panfishing excursions, we'll select a model with at least three built-in seats—one on the front, one at the rear, and one in the middle. That leaves two open deck compartments where we can place platforms and perhaps mount pedestal seats. A bow platform can be easily installed on a semi-v craft. To modify the between-seat compartments, we could drop in two sheets of $^1/_2$-inch marine plywood cut to fit the floor in each compartment. Then, we could cover each sheet with indoor/outdoor carpeting to cut down on excessive noise, before mounting our pedestal seats to the boards. Use pedestals that can be removed from the base mount just in case you want to take the seats out at times. The plywood will remain unattached as well, so it can be removed for cleaning the boat and to eliminate excess weight when needed.

Livewells are another add-on we should consider. They're nice, but they're expensive, too. Since panfish will fit and keep nicely in a wire fish basket, we'll go that route instead and cut our fishing equipment costs.

Outboard Motors

Outboards may cost more than the boat they power. But since we'll be traveling fairly long distances on some of the waters we fish, and since wind and current may occasionally be strong, we'll definitely want an outboard on our ultimate panfish boat.

The motor we select should have sufficient horsepower to properly power our boat but shouldn't be so large that it exceeds the safe limit established by the boat's manufacturer. Never exceed these maximum horsepower ratings, since overpowered boats are unsafe.

Console and stick steering provide better forward vision for motoring from one spot to another, but budget limitations put these luxury options beyond reach of most panfishermen. Tiller-operated outboards, which offer excellent control and maneuverability, are a less expensive option which is well-suited to most panfishing situations.

Taking these things into consideration, we'll power our boat using a 15-horsepower outboard with tiller steering. That's adequate to move our ultimate panfish boat from point A to point B

Sunfish, as well as crappies, often will hang tight around thick brush and cover so fishing brushy points and other thick woody cover thoroughly can produce nice stringers of panfish.

The Ultimate Panfish Boat 63

on a lake or river safely, quickly and economically.

Electric Motors

Electric, or trolling, motors are less powerful than outboards, but they are also much quieter and less likely to spook jittery fish. We'll want one to move our boat slowly through the fishing area while we fish. We'll also use this motor as our main power source on small waters where an outboard isn't needed or isn't permitted.

Foot-controlled models free your hands for casting and playing fish, but these are usually more expensive, and most must be permanently mounted to the bow. An electric motor with clamp-on mounts and tiller steering works fine for most panfishing, so that's what we'll select. Due to space and budget limitations, we'll choose a 12-volt motor powered by a single deep-cycle battery, in-

During the winter in Southern waters, sunfish often will be found in deep water. These anglers are fishing a deep creek channel that is bordered by standing timber.

Easy trailering makes any number of waters accessible to the panfish fisherman. Running lights, electric trolling motor, depthfinder and small anchor are helpful accessories.

stead of a 24-volt motor that requires two batteries. A model with 28 pounds thrust and a 30-inch shaft length should push or pull our boat quite well.

Trailers

It's possible to get by without a boat trailer if you drive a pickup. But by using a trailer, we can cut down dramatically on launching and take-out time, thus leaving more time for fishing. Using a trailer also frees up space in the back of the pickup for hauling camping gear, food and other items needed for extended fishing trips.

We don't need anything fancy, so we'll select a lightweight aluminum or steel frame trailer that will safely carry the 12-foot johnboat. The trailer should also have a good bow rope winch and rollers on the frame. We'll also throw in a sturdy strap to secure the boat to the trailer, and a grease gun to keep the wheel bearings well lubricated.

Sonar

Some anglers consider a sonar unit (depthfinder or depth

Life jackets, like this model from Stearns which inflates from a CO_2 cartridge with the pull of a cord, makes boating and wading safe. The jacket can also be inflated by blowing into a hose located under a top pocket. A portable marine fire extinguisher is a smart addition to any boat, and a floating, halogen flashlight should be kept ready for emergencies.

sounder) an unnecessary option. But many anglers know how important this piece of equipment can be when trying to locate fish concentrations. Since we're using a relatively small boat where space is at a premium, we'll purchase a portable unit that can be positioned where we want it each trip. A portable can also be stored outside our boat when not needed. We want a model that will at least indicate water depth, the configuration of bottom cover and structure, and the location of fish. These are standard features on many reasonably priced units.

Accessories

To make our fishing trips more comfortable and productive, we could add some inexpensive, yet important, accessories. First, we'll want a small mushroom anchor and anchor line on each end of the boat, so we can maintain position on breezy days. Since we'll also be trolling for crappies and other panfish on occasion, we could add some rod holders as well.

Also important are a battery box for storing the 12-volt trolling motor battery, and a good fuel container for the outboard.

Our boat should also be properly supplied with safety and

emergency equipment that's kept in constant readiness.

We'll always have an approved life jacket on board for each passenger, and insist that everyone wear one! There should also be rain gear and warm clothes on board in case of inclement weather, and a fire extinguisher, since ours is a gas-powered craft. Non-skid strips provide safe footing when moving about the boat.

We may sometimes fish at night, so we'll want to mount running lights, and we'll carry a flashlight or spotlight to signal our presence to other boaters.

We'll carry a tool kit for emergency repairs, including extra shear pins, a couple of paddles or oars, too, so we won't be stranded if our motor quits. And we'll attach long ropes on the bow and stern that can be used if we need a tow or a handy tie-up.

To be on the safe side, we'll also carry a small survival kit that includes waterproof matches, a sound signal (whistle or air horn), a map and compass (know how to use them!), and high-energy snacks, just in case we get stranded or lost.

Summary

So there we have it. Our ultimate panfish boat is a 12- to 14-foot, narrow, three- or four-seat, aluminum, semi-v boat, or semi-v bow johnboat. We've improved comfort and quietness, and saved some money, by adding our own removable pedestal seats and carpeted decks. We'll power our craft with a 15-horsepower, tiller-operated outboard and a 12-volt, 28-pound thrust electric motor. We'll transport our boat on a lightweight, aluminum or steel frame trailer, and we've added a portable sonar unit, anchors, and a wide array of safety and emergency equipment to make our fishing trips more safe, enjoyable and productive.

Sunfish

5

Sunfishing's Big Three

S unfish are the most abundant, most caught, most varied, most colorful, most loved sportfish in America. Named for their bright, sunny colors, these bantam panfish are widely known as *bream*, a name that originated with early settlers who thought they resembled a flat-bodied European fish of the same name.

By numbers caught and anglers who catch them, sunfish are the most important freshwater fish in the country by a long shot. No wonder! They have all the qualities to put them at the head of the list. They are available throughout the 48 contiguous states, from Maine to California, from Florida to Washington, and all points in between. They are extremely prolific and thus generally abundant. They are aggressive, which complements their willingness to bite, and very social, which translates into fast-paced fishing fun. They are astonishingly beautiful, put up a battle all out of proportion to their size, and they are, without a doubt, among the tastiest fish on earth.

Fishing for sunfish is an excellent way to introduce youngsters to the joys of panfishing, because even simple techniques can pull 'em in. But don't fall for the elitists' inference that they are just "kids' fish." Angling for "sunnies" is a wonderful pastime everybody can enjoy. There's no need for fancy boats that could bankrupt a banana republic—no magforce, powerbuster rods, jet-dashboard reels and suitcase-sized tackle boxes full of expensive lures. Quite the contrary.

Earthworms always are a good choice for enticing bluegills and other sunfish into hooking themselves, whether used alone or in tandem with other live or artificial baits.

Sunfishing's Big Three

Worms, crickets and tiny lures are the sunfish's blue-plate specials. Cane poles, cut-rate rods and reels, and paint-bare johnboats can replace the snazzy gear. Glamorous? Hardly. But who cares. Sunfish provide much-needed relief from what too many folks nowadays consider "serious" fishing, with its multitudinous gadgets, endless harangues and wearisome technicalities. If you'll let them, sunfish can lead you back to what fishing is supposed to be—plain, relaxing, out-and-out fun.

The sunfish, of which there are more than 30 species, belong to the family Centrarchidae, the sunfish family. This family also includes the white and black crappies, the rock bass and the warmouth, all of which are discussed later in this book. However, this chapter, and the next, will include only the true sunfish, members of the genus *Lepomis*. We'll begin in this chapter by discussing the "Big Three" of sunfishing—the bluegill, redear and redbreast sunfish. In the next chapter, we'll take a look at several smaller, but still sporty and very popular, gamefish like the green sunfish, the longear sunfish, the pumpkinseed and the spotted sunfish.

Bluegills: The All-American Panfish

The bluegill (Lepomis macrochirus) is a fish so popular, so well-studied, and so varied in its habits, it could easily be the subject of an entire book. Prolific and pugnacious, this spunky tyke meets just about all the requirements necessary to rank as a great sportfish. It was originally found only in the eastern half of the United States, but stocking has expanded its range to include every state but Alaska. Bluegills are now the most widespread and abundant sunfish species in the country. They are also the most popular. In fact, by numbers caught, this sporty customer is unquestionably our nation's top gamefish.

Bluegill Facts

Bluegills have more nicknames than a boy named William. Most folks simply call them "bream." But in some parts of the country, they may be dubbed coppernose bream, blue sunfish, perch, sun perch, copperheads, dollardees, pond perch, gold perch, blue joes or 'gills. Most of these names originated in the rural South.

These colorful panfish are quite gregarious, often living in loose schools of up to 20 or 30 individuals. They adapt quite well

Bluegill

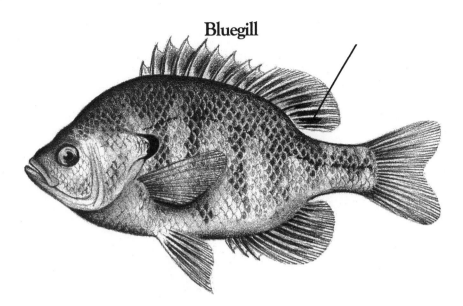

Popular and widespread, bluegills can be identified by their yellow to orange belly, bluish cheeks, all black gill-cover lobe and dark blotch on rear of dorsal fin.

to a variety of water types and conditions, and within their range, they inhabit everything from tiny farm ponds, crystal-clear creeks and sluggish bayous to cypress-shrouded oxbow lakes (lakes formed in delta areas where a river channel has moved), vast man-made impoundments and broad lowland rivers. They thrive best in warm, clear waters and frequent areas where aquatic plants, brush, timber and other cover are present. Their living requirements are similar to those of largemouth bass, and where one species is common, the other is likely to be common, too.

The tiny mouth, entirely black "ear flaps," and sky-blue throat are this sunfish's distinguishing characteristics. The pectoral fin is long and pointed, and there's a dark blotch at the rear of the soft dorsal fin on adult fish.

Coloration varies considerably, running all the way from nearly black or dark purple to dark brown, green or yellowish-silver, with emerald and brassy reflections. The dusky vertical bars usually displayed on the sides of the silvery juveniles may be vague or absent on older specimens. Breeding males have spectacularly bright colors, the head and throat vivid aqua to blue, and the breast a brilliant copper to bright orange-red. Females usually

Bluegills can be found in every state of the nation and in parts of Mexico and Canada. The exceptions are parts of the Colorado and Montana Rockies.

have a yellow breast and are less brightly hued.

Even a big bluegill has a tiny mouth. Larger adults occasionally eat small fish and crayfish, but bluegills feed predominantly on tiny animals—primarily insects, insect larvae and nymphs, snails, worms and other small invertebrates.

Bluegill Size

Although they reach the heaviest weight of any true sunfish, bluegills seldom exceed 10 inches or 1 pound in size. A population of adult fish in habitat conducive to good growth will usually have many 6- to 8-inch fish weighing 4 to 8 ounces apiece, with a smattering of 10- to 12-inch individuals at a pound or better. They grow as much in girth as they do in length, and the real heavyweights, a pound and up, resemble—in size and shape—the dinner plate they frequently end up on. The largest bluegill ever taken on hook-and-line, a fish caught in 1950 in Alabama's Ketona Lake, weighed 4 pounds, 12 ounces, was 15 inches long, and had a girth of 18.25 inches.

Anything bluegills lack in size, they more than adequately compensate for with their sheer numbers. In fact, they are so prolific that overharvest is seldom ever a problem, or even a possibility. In fact, underharvest is much more likely. Overabundant

You really don't have to worry about having different techniques for different panfish because the same approach in waters where several different species live can lead to hefty stringers.

Sunfishing's Big Three

bluegills are common in many waters, especially unmanaged ponds. Not only do they deserve more angling attention, they often require it.

Bluegill Spawning Behavior

Bluegills begin spawning when the water temperature reaches 67 to 70 degrees F. In Florida and other southern latitudes, this may be as early as late March. In the northernmost states, spawning may not start until late June. The peak of bedding activity is usually during the early part of the spawning season, but some fish will be on nests as late as July and August.

Males build the nests, usually on a sand or gravel bottom in shallow-water cover. Silt and debris are swept away with the body and tail to create a nest 2 to 4 inches deep and approximately a foot in diameter. There may be many nests side by side in a small area, each of which appears as a light-colored circle when viewed from above. Prime spawning sites in clear water look like artillery impact areas when bluegills are on their nests.

When spawning nears, the male hovers over the nest bowl and circles its rim. Females, swollen with eggs, swim in from deeper water and are gently guided to the nests by the males. Then, if the female is receptive, eggs and milt are released, and the 12,000 to 60,000 eggs are fertilized.

The male constantly guards the nest and keeps the eggs aerated and clean by gently fanning them with his fins. Under normal weather conditions, the eggs will hatch within two to five days. The male stays on the nest until the eggs hatch but does not guard the fry.

Bluegills are highly vulnerable to predation during their first months of life. But if they survive and adequate food is available, they can grow to 3 inches or more and become sexually mature in one year. Early maturity, tremendous reproductive potential, and an average 3- to 4-year life span can combine to create an overpopulation problem that affects the entire fish community.

The Bluegill/Bassin' Connection

Anglers, too, play an important role in bluegill overabundance. Bass are the fisherman's primary quarry on many ponds and small lakes populated with bluegills. And since bass are the bluegill's main predator, excessive bass harvest removes a vital,

Redear Sunfish

Commonly known as the shellcracker, the redear is the fastest growing of the true sunfish. The redear has light green to gold sides and a black gill cover tipped with a bright red fringe.

built-in check on the bluegill population. Too little predation causes bluegill numbers to increase to a level where not enough food exists for each fish to sustain normal growth. This results in numerous stunted bluegills, and these overabundant bait-stealers give bluegills a bad rap as a quality sportfish.

In reality, however, it's the overuse of the bass resource that actually hurts both the bluegill and bass populations. The stunted, overly plentiful bluegills begin preying on bass eggs and newly hatched fry. This means fewer bass reach maturity, and thus, there are fewer predators to feed on the bluegills. That means still fewer bass and so on and so on. It's a vicious circle that can only be broken by proper fisheries management.

Good management helps establish and maintain a proper balance between sunfish and bass. For every pound of bass taken from a small body of water, biologists suggest that 8 to 10 pounds of bluegills or other sunfish also be removed. Therefore, the ardent bluegill fisherman is really the bass angler's best friend.

The Redear Sunfish: A Heavyweight Contender
If sunfish were placed in divisions like boxers, the red-eared

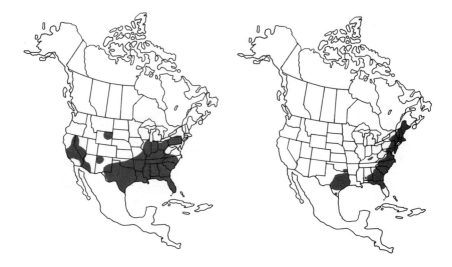

Redear sunfish are found throughout the Southeastern United States and in parts of a few Western states including California. The redbreast has a much more limited distribution.

sunfish (Lepomis microlophus) would be a heavyweight contender. The largest of the true sunfishes, this spunky panfish delivers a knockout punch that will put your bobber down for the 10 count. It's one of the finest fighters for its size in freshwater, and during late spring and early summer, ardent panfishermen swarm to prime redear waters to get in on the year's best action.

Redears aren't as colorful as bluegills, but they are handsome fish, nevertheless. The back is usually olive-green, fading to silvery-green sides that are often checkered with brown or green mottling. A yellow wash colors the belly on most adult fish. The mouth is small, and the pectoral fins are long and pointed.

The "redear" name is a practical designation based on the color of the ear flaps at the rear edge of the gill plates. Bluegills have flaps that are entirely blue or black. On adult redears, the black ear flaps have a reddish, crescent-shaped border. Males are more brightly colored than females and sport a bright, cherry-red border. Females and young usually have a pale orange border. The pumpkinseed is the only similar sunfish with bright red on the ear flap, but redears lack the iridescent blue-green facial bars of their sunfish "cousin," the pumpkinseed.

Complete Angler's Library

Another redear characteristic is the set of flattened grinding teeth in the throat. These allow redears to crunch the shells of the tiny mollusks that form most of their diet and prompted the common nickname "shellcracker." Other frequently used redear monickers include improved, government-improved or GI bream, yellow bream, chinquapin, stumpknocker, branch perch, pond perch and cherry gill.

Sizable Quarry

Size is the redear's most unique attraction. Two pounds is exceptionally large for most sunfish, but some southern lakes produce $1^1/_2$- to 2-pound shellcrackers with astounding regularity. Redears over 3 pounds have been reported in California, Georgia, Kentucky, Ohio, South Carolina, Tennessee and Texas. And anglers in Florida, Alabama, Virginia and North Carolina have caught redears topping 4 pounds. The all-tackle world record from Florida's Merritt's Mill Pond—a lake that has produced several state and world records—weighed an astounding 4 pounds, 13 ounces. Redears usually average 8 to 10 inches in length and about half a pound in weight.

Though native to the Southeastern U.S.—Florida, Georgia, South Carolina, Tennessee, Mississippi, Alabama, Arkansas, Louisiana, and parts of Texas, Oklahoma, Missouri, Kentucky, Illinois and North Carolina—the redear now thrives in many other areas where it has been introduced. Its range now also includes most of Pennsylvania, Ohio and Indiana, and portions of Virginia, West Virginia, California, Nevada, Arizona, New Mexico and Wyoming. Within its range, however, the redear is usually much more restricted than the bluegill. For instance, in Arkansas, one of the country's prime territories for big redears, bluegills are considered major sportfish in 97 percent of the state's major public fishing waters; redears rank high in only 60 percent.

Quality Stockers

Redears are a popular choice for stocking farm ponds and lakes, for several reasons. They are less prolific than the bluegill, and, therefore, less likely to be stunted by overpopulation. They also grow more rapidly and attain a larger size than bluegills from the same water. Like the bluegill, they have sweet, flaky, white flesh, but redears can be kept for the frying pan at a smaller size because of the plumpness of their bodies.

Bottom Dwellers

Redears have a definite preference for warm, clear waters with no noticeable current. They tend to congregate around stumps, roots, logs, standing timber and green aquatic vegetation. They live and feed mostly on the bottom, and prefer deeper water than most other sunfish, sometimes moving to depths of 20 to 30 feet in the summer. Small snails, clams, mussels, worms, insect larvae and other bottom-dwelling creatures make up most of their diet, but redears also eat insects and other foods.

Spawning Traits

During the big beddings of spring and early summer, redears are extremely sociable and jam up in gigantic colonies to carry out their mating ritual. Bedding areas of $^1/_4$ acre and even $^1/_2$ acre in size are found on many lakes, but the average colony is about the size of a one-car to three-car parking space. They like to nest in lily pads, usually in two to eight feet of water, but you can find them most anywhere you'd find bluegills—around stumps and logs, cypress trees, brush or even on open sand and gravel bottoms. Bedding areas are well-established in most redear lakes, and the fish usually return to the same spots year after year.

Spawning begins as early as March in southern Florida where many first-rate redear lakes are located. April and May are prime months in most other southern states, while northern parts of the redear's range may see spawning peaks in May and June. Some shellcrackers spawn into August and September.

The redear's major activity periods during the spawning season are thought by many anglers to be closely linked to periods of the full moon. Most experienced redear rustlers will tell you feeding activity peaks from three days before the full moon until three days after. Between these periods, fishing takes a nosedive until the next phase stimulates further activity. This observation is totally unscientific, but experience shows that checking the moon and calendar, and using a fishing strategy that takes advantage of this presumed scenario, will help you catch more redears.

The Redbreast Sunfish: No. 3 On The Sunfish Pop Chart

The redbreast sunfish hasn't gleaned as much press as its larger

Redbreast Sunfish

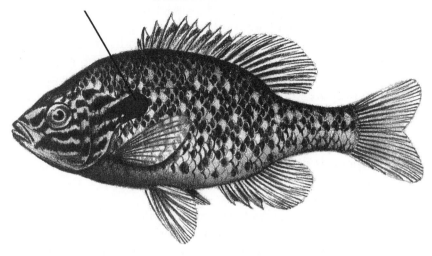

Redbreast sunfish gill-cover lobes may be as long as those of longear sunfish, but the redbreast's lobe is entirely black. They are sometimes called "robin" because of their bright, red belly.

cousins, the bluegill and redear, but this feisty little sunfish fights tenaciously and is held in high esteem in areas where it is common. It is one of the largest sunfishes and frequently attains weights of one-half to three-quarters of a pound in prime waters. Most large specimens are caught in the Southeast, from the Carolinas down into Florida. The all-tackle world record—a real whopper at 2 pounds, 1 ounce—was taken from Florida's Suwannee River, a stream where 1-pound redbreasts hardly raise an eyebrow. In other parts of its range, even large ones seldom exceed half a pound.

Identifying Redbreasts

The redbreast is a strikingly colored fish with a moderate-sized mouth and short, rounded pectoral fins. Males usually have an olive-green back and sides, with bronze flecking on the scales. The head is streaked with short, wavy lines of turquoise. Females are less brightly colored but are basically the same hues.

The "redbreast" name is derived from the bright splash of color across the breast and part of the belly. However, a redbreast's breast is not always red. On some fish, it is vivid yellow or rust.

This sunfish's most infallible identification marks are its extremely long ear flaps. These are typically solid black, and those on male fish are usually longer and broader than those on females. The longear sunfish also has long, black ear flaps, but on longears, the flaps usually have a whitish border (vs. no light border).

Though "redbreast sunfish" is the official common name, this sunfish goes by a variety of interesting regional names as well. The most common are yellowbelly sunfish and yellowbreast sunfish. Others include robin, red-headed bream, red perch, tobacco box, leather ear, black-eared pondfish, hornear, and longear (a confusion with the true longear sunfish). The "red" and "yellow" designations represent differing coloration from different waters.

Transplanting Redbreasts

The redbreast's original range extended through the Atlantic Coast states from Maine to central Florida. It was later transplanted into several areas outside its native range, including parts of Kentucky, Arkansas, Oklahoma, Texas and Alabama.

In some regions, portions of Texas for instance, introductions were highly successful, and the redbreast has become an established and highly popular sportfish. But other states, like Arkansas, were unable to establish breeding populations, and stockings were discontinued.

Today, populations are scattered, and the species is less common, as one moves westward from Florida. In Texas, at the far-western edge of their range, one must be quite selective in the choice of fishing waters to catch redbreasts. Certain waters have great numbers of them, while others have none.

Redbreasts Are Stream Dwellers

Redbreasts thrive in diverse waters, everything from cold mountain streams to warm lakes and ponds and brackish coastal marshes. They are, however, primarily stream dwellers in most of their range. From Virginia northward, they are often found in smallmouth bass streams. Other regions find them inhabiting warm, slow-moving rivers like Florida's Suwannee and crystal-clear creeks like those in the central Texas Hill Country. They flourish in the company of other sunfishes and are found in many lakes, ponds and streams where bluegills, redears and other sunfish are found in abundance.

In streams, redbreasts are usually found in deep pools out of fast current. They often hide behind boulders and logs and in undercut banks around tree roots. In lakes and ponds, they prefer deep, weedy areas with sand or mud bottoms.

Redbreasts feed primarily on snails, small crayfish, aquatic and terrestrial insects, and insect larvae, and unlike bluegills and redears, small fish also make up a large part of the diet. Like redear sunfish, redbreasts are primarily bottom-feeders.

Late Spawners

Redbreasts spawn somewhat later than other common sunfishes. In Florida, the peak spawning season is around mid-April. Middle Atlantic states see a peak around June, and New England redbreasts may not bed until July. In southern latitudes, spawning may continue throughout the summer.

Redbreasts are often solitary nesters, bedding close to shore near logs, stumps and snags in one and one-half to five feet of water. Sandy bottoms are favored, and the nests are usually large—up to 3 feet in diameter and 6 to 8 inches deep.

Slack-water areas where cypress trees, sand and gravel bars, snags and other structures break the current are favored nesting sites in rivers. Males are very protective of the eggs and fry, and lures or baits worked over the beds are quickly attacked. Like largemouth bass, released male redbreasts return to guard their nest and can be caught again.

Anglers should also know that redbreasts are more prone to feed at night than other sunfish. Catching them on natural baits or noisy lures after dark is one of sunfishing's most unique thrills.

6

The Other Sunfish

luegills, redears and redbreasts are the prima donnas of the sunfish clan, but many other sunnies also exhibit excellent sporting qualities. Most of these "other" sunfish are quite small, averaging only a few ounces apiece. But fishermen who measure the success of a fishing trip by numbers of fish caught, instead of the size of fish caught, will find these little beauties much to their liking.

Longear Sunfish: The Rainbow Warrior

It would be hard to imagine a fish of any sort more beautiful than the longear sunfish. This gorgeous little creature is emblazoned with a rainbow of colors—aquamarine back and sides with gold and emerald speckles, a face of green or tangerine, a lemon-yellow to orange belly, and opalescent veins of turquoise striping the cheeks, nose and gill covers. Males are even more brilliantly colored than the gaudy females, especially during the spawning season when the breast turns cherry red or fiery orange. Both sexes sport long, black, white-edged ear flaps that protrude from the gill covers like ebony earrings.

Beauty isn't the longear's only gratifying attribute. This little buster is an aggressive, doughty warrior, too, and on the table, it is delectable. Yet most panfish anglers busy with bluegills, crappies or other fish pay it little mind. When someone catches one, it's usually deplored as too small and tossed back. That's regrettable, for this handsome sunfish is an unsung delight that can render

This stringer is mostly longear sunfish with a few bluegills thrown in for good measure. While panfish, particularly longears, may be small, a mess like this will feed a family of four.

The Other Sunfish

countless hours of angling enjoyment.

The longear sunfish (Lepomis megalotis) goes by a variety of colloquial names—names like sun perch, cherry bream, pumpkin-seed, creek bream, red-eyed sunfish and tobacco box, the latter in reference to its long ear flaps that are sometimes rounded like the lid of a tobacco tin. It is said to be most common in the mid-South—Arkansas, Kentucky, Tennessee, Mississippi and southern Missouri. Its entire range, however, is actually quite expansive, stretching from Lake Superior to the south Texas Gulf Coast, and from the middle Atlantic states west through Oklahoma and into New Mexico.

The scant references you will find on the longear invariably describe it as a fish of crystal-clear creeks and small, gravel-bottomed rivers. It is, indeed, a characteristic inhabitant of these types of waters within its range, but this rainbow warrior is anything but a specialist restricted to a narrow range of habitats. Longears are native to and quite abundant in oxbow lakes, meandering delta rivers, bayous and other lowland waters, and they have adapted quite well to life in all sorts of man-made impoundments. In fact, it is difficult to find any type of freshwater fishing hole where a longear couldn't thrive. Warm or cold, big or small, deep or shallow—if it's not too polluted, longears will call it home.

Longears vary in appearance geographically, and one shouldn't expect a specimen from a Pennsylvania smallmouth stream to look the same as one from an Arkansas bayou, any more than you might expect a Georgia belle to speak with a Brooklyn accent. In some Eastern states, the longear's entire body is blue, green and yellow. Arkansas' longears have vivid blue streaks and orange spots on the body. Regardless of regional variations, though, if you catch a sunfish more brightly colored than any you've ever seen, it's probably a longear.

In 1985, a 1-pound, 12-ounce longear from Elephant Butte Lake, New Mexico, achieved world-record status. But finding a longear that weighs even 1 pound is about as likely as winning a state lottery. Three to 5 ounces is probably about the size of an average adult, with anything topping that can easily be granted instant "trophy" status.

Their diminutive stature shouldn't deter you from fishing for longears, though. Some waters are literally swarming with 4- to 6-inchers, and many folks would readily agree that catching lots of

Longear Sunfish

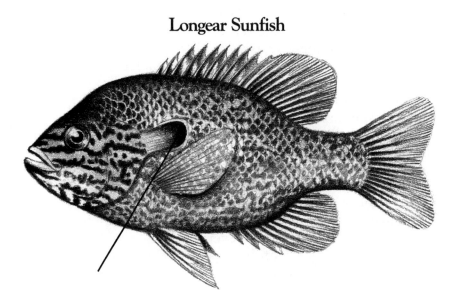

The longear sunfish can be identified by its bright orange and blue spots and strong streaking and worming on the gill cover as well as the long gill-cover lobe fringed with a lighter color.

little guys is better than catching few or no bigger fish. Longears aren't especially shy, and it's common to see several chasing a lure.

On small rivers and creeks, longears frequent shallow- to medium-depth pools and slow runs with scarcely perceptible current. They seem especially fond of steep, rocky ledges and undercut banks out of stiff flow. In oxbow lakes and lowland streams, longears usually hang out near cypress knees, half-submerged horizontal logs and other types of sizable woody cover. Lake and pond fish seem to concentrate around weedbed edges, steeply sloping rock or gravel banks, and quite frequently, around fishing piers, docks and similar structures. They feed primarily on insects and small fish, and usually spawn over gravel in brush-free areas.

Regardless of how you fish for them, if you want to sample the bounty of longear fishing, you'll probably have to alter your current standard for "keeping size." Most longears you'll land probably won't resemble anything you've ever called a keeper before, but even the 4- and 5-inchers pack two surprisingly thick fillets on their tiny skeletons. Dress these mini-panfish, salt and pepper to taste, and roll in yellow cornmeal. Then fry them for a minute or so—no longer—in vegetable or peanut oil heated to 350 degrees

F. Strip out the dorsal fin, pull the two flaky white fillets away from the bones on each side, and settle yourself down to enjoy one of Mother Nature's finest treats.

One further suggestion: be sure to catch a lot!

Green Sunfish: The Prolific Pioneer

Of all the sunfish species, none is more abundant and adaptable than the green sunfish. This colorful little sprite is a prolific colonizer tolerant of warm, turbid water. It is a pioneering species, readily populating new bodies of water, and is among the first fish to repopulate streams after periods of drought.

No creek is too small for it, no river too large. Turn its stream into a lake or pond, and it will stick around and do just fine, thank you. In fact, if a body of water is even remotely capable of supporting fish life, the green sunfish (Lepomis cyanellus) is likely to be there. "Ubiquitous" is perhaps the best way to describe it.

If you've never seen a green sunfish, you've probably never fished freshwater. It occurs in virtually every body of freshwater in the continental United States and is one of the easiest fish to add to your stringer.

Green Sunfish

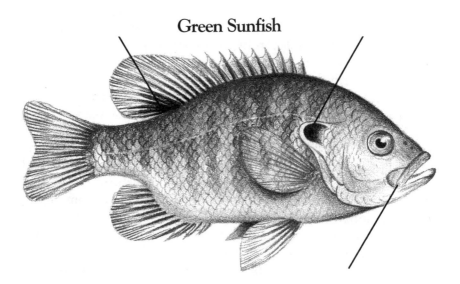

Green sunfish have a long body and large mouth. As on the bluegill, there is a dark blotch at the base of the dorsal, but the green's gill-cover lobe has a light margin.

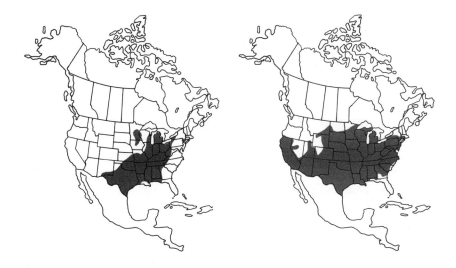

The longear sunfish (left) is found primarily in the East-Central and Southeastern states while the green sunfish (right) is found in nearly all of the states except the Pacific Northwest.

The green sunfish is like an old acquaintance you run into at the supermarket—you may recognize the face but can't place the name. Few fish have such a variety of colloquial names. Some folks know it as the black perch, shade perch, blue-spotted sunfish, ricefield slick or rubbertail. In other locales, green perch, goggle-eye, branch perch, blue bass and buffalo sunfish are commonly used nicknames. You'll seldom ever hear an angler talking about catching a green sunfish, though. "Perch" or "goggle-eye" maybe, but not green sunfish.

Regardless of what you call it, the green sunfish is a gutsy little fighter worthy of your attention. It always seems to be hungry or mad at the world, looking for a fight. It's not exactly an angling challenge. In fact, the simile "shooting fish in a barrel" might have been coined to describe fishing for green sunfish. But on ultra-light tackle, this adaptable little devil makes quite a showing of itself. It has a "no fooling" strike, and if you've never sampled deep-fried green sunfish fillets, you've missed a real treat.

Green sunfish are long, robust fish with a big mouth like a bass. The back and sides are usually olive to bluish green, the undersides are yellow-orange, the short ear flaps are black with white or yellow-orange margins, and the cheeks have distinctive worm-like blue squiggles. The pectoral fins are short and rounded, and the tips of the pelvic, anal and tail fins are often a yellow to orange color. The young have dark, closely spaced bars on the sides.

"Greenies" are often found in quiet pools of rivers or creeks and along shorelines of lakes and ponds. Small creeks incapable of supporting other sportfish often yield good stringers of hand-size green sunfish. Spawning usually occurs in shallow backwaters over bottoms of gravel, clay or detritus.

They eat a variety of foods, including insects (both aquatic and terrestrial), crayfish and small fish, and are almost always found near some type of cover. It could be a root wad, weedbed, brushpile or logjam. Maybe boulders or rocks in a stream, or riprap along the face of dam. Even the shade of an overhanging tree will do. If there's cover, green sunfish will be there.

Their only major flaw, in terms of angling quality, is size. Adults can grow 8 to 10 inches long and reach a pound in weight, but even that size is unusual. Unless they become overpopulated and stunted (a frequent problem in small ponds and lakes), most will run around 4 to 8 ounces. The all-tackle world record from Stockton Lake in Missouri was a true heavyweight weighing in at 2 pounds, 2 ounces.

Pumpkinseeds are found farther north than any of the other true sunfish. They are absent from much of Florida and all of the South-western U.S.

Complete Angler's Library

Pumpkinseed

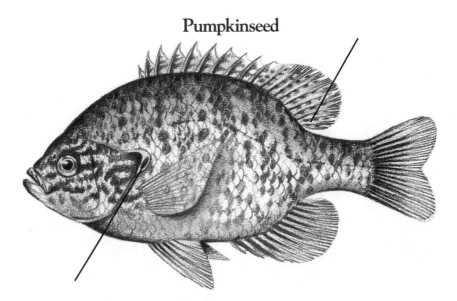

The pumpkinseed has faint, dark vertical bars on its golden sides. Its cheeks often show bright blue worming. The gill-cover lobe has a red spot at its tip. Dorsal spot is absent.

Judge the green sunfish for what it is, not what it looks like. Sure, it may be a tad on the small side. But it's also widespread, abundant, hard-hitting, fun to catch and excellent on the table. The green sunfish is an applaudably aggressive citizen of waters throughout the country. So applaud it ... catch it ... eat it!

The Pumpkinseed: Panfishing's Little Jewel

Of the pumpkinseed, Henry David Thoreau once wrote: "It is a very beautiful and compact fish, perfect in all its parts, looking like a brilliant coin fresh from the mint." Indeed, this panfishing favorite is uncommonly beautiful, displaying silvery green sides with orange and red flecks and iridescent blue and emerald reflections. The underside is gold to orange-red, and streaks of aqua radiate from the nose back across the face. The black ear flaps have whitish margins and a splash of vivid red at the tip. The female is likewise marked, but her colors are more subdued.

The "pumpkinseed" name is derived not from the orange spots speckling the sides, but rather from the shape of the body which resembles the outline of a pumpkin seed. "Common sunfish" is a moniker frequently hung on it, and in some areas, it also goes by

Giant pumpkinseed? You bet! When you find sunfish this size, keep the spot to yourself. It doesn't take long for a group of anglers to remove all the trophy fish from a small lake.

such names as kivvy, yellowbelly, round sunfish, sunny, roach, quiver and sun bass.

Unlike many sunfish species which reach their greatest sizes and numbers in southern waters, the pumpkinseed (Lepomis gibbosus) is primarily a fish of northern lakes, ponds and streams. Its original range extended from southern Canada, the Great Lakes states and New England down through the Atlantic Coast states as far south as Georgia. It has now been transplanted to many western areas far outside its indigenous domain, and is frequently encountered in the cool waters of the Pacific Northwest, California, Montana, Wyoming, Idaho and Colorado.

Pumpkinseeds prefer quiet, clear lakes and streams with stands of aquatic vegetation. They generally live in cooler waters than most other true sunfish, and tend to inhabit thicker vegetation than bluegills and redears. They are less prolific than bluegills, laying only 1,000 to 3,000 eggs once a year, compared to the tens of thousands of eggs a single bluegill may produce several times annually. Thus, in waters where bluegills and pumpkinseeds compete for living space, the bluegill usually outnumbers its cousin.

Though thick and chunky, most of these sprightly little gamesters are smaller than bluegills, and a half-pounder is a true whopper. The world-record, a real giant at 1 pound, 6 ounces, was caught in Oswego Pond, New York, in 1985.

The pumpkinseed's habits and life history are similar in many respects to those of the redear sunfish. Like its southern counterpart, this bantam sunfish depends heavily on snails, small mollusks and insects for food and usually feeds on or near the bottom. Nesting occurs at about the same time as the redear and is like that of other small sunfish.

One of the nicest things about pumpkinseeds is their propensity for pronounced winter activity. Ice fishing is almost as productive as spring angling, especially when using meal worms, maggots, catalpa worms and other small larvae for bait.

The Spotted Sunfish: A Southern Treat

Though it's not a very well-known fish, the spotted sunfish (Lepomis punctatus) is distributed throughout the Southeast, from eastern Texas through the Florida peninsula and north along the Atlantic slope to southeastern North Carolina. It is also found in the Mississippi River basin, from Louisiana north to Illinois. It seldom exceeds a few ounces in weight, but its consistent scrappiness, pretty colors, chunky physique and flavorful, sweet-tasting meat make it a favorite with panfishermen in many areas, especially in Florida. Few anglers fish purposely for it, but as an incidental in a mixed bag, there's no reason to keep it off the stringer.

Primarily a resident of streams and oxbow lakes in the lowlands, the "spotted bream" or "stumpknocker" as it is best known, prefers quiet or sluggish, clear waters with abundant aquatic vegetation and other cover. In the few upland streams it penetrates, it often frequents quiet, willow-lined pools. Its spawning habits are similar to other sunfish, but it is primarily a solitary nester.

Spotted sunfish can usually be distinguished by the dense longitudinal rows of reddish-orange (males) or yellow (females) spots that speckle the dark blue or olive sides. But some fish in Florida,

Georgia and other Deep South states are marked with brown, blue or black spots instead of red or yellow. The face and head are usually dark, with a pale red area just above the gill flap. The undersides are yellowish to dusky white, and the short ear flap is black with a white or pale yellow margin.

Spotted sunfish are usually found in calm or moderately flowing water, usually near some type of woody or rocky cover. They often hide around cypress knees in oxbows, and around boulders, fallen trees and small eddies in streams. From these spots they attack small crayfish, insects and other frequently-taken foods. In the tidal streams of Florida, one of the best stumpknocker states, spotted sunfish hang out in deep holes beneath undercut banks waiting to attack small crabs, shrimp and other invertebrates.

Unfortunately, it's a rare occasion when you'll take more than one or two individuals from a single patch of cover. That's one of the reasons this sunfish is so little known. But despite its relative obscurity and small size, the just-plain-pugnacious spotted sunfish is a real treat for any fun-seeking angler.

Hybrid Sunfish

Natural hybridization or "crossbreeding" between various species of sunfish is common. In fact, all the popular sunfish are known to cross with other species of sunfish.

This usually occurs where one species of sunfish is abundant and the other is rare. For example, in waters densely populated with bluegills yet sparsely inhabited by pumpkinseeds, the pumpkinseeds may spawn with their more abundant cousins. If redears are common, and there are few longears, these species may hybridize, producing a redear/longear cross. Under similar circumstances, almost any two species of sunfish are likely to crossbreed.

Hybrid sunfish, which are often misidentified, are typically intermediate in color, proportions and whatever other ways the parent species differ. For instance, a green sunfish/bluegill hybrid, a common natural occurrence, might have a moderately sized mouth that falls between the very large mouth of the green sunfish and the very small mouth of the bluegill. This hybrid exhibits colors of both parents, and is often confused with green sunfish, bluegills, warmouths and redears.

Some hybrids are propagated for stocking, because they exhibit rapid growth, generally good vigor, lower fertility and high catchability. Hybrids can be especially good for stocking ponds that are too small to support a balance of predators and prey. The hybrid's inferior reproductive capacity keeps numbers low, and individual fish are usually larger as a result.

One of the most successful hatchery-made hybrids is the green sunfish/bluegill cross which is often known as the super-bream, Georgia giant, or simply hybrid bream. These are scrappy, aggressive fish that hit bait hard, fight respectably, and often reach 1 $\frac{1}{2}$ to 2 pounds in weight. Tests show that 95 percent of this hybrid's offspring are male, a fact that helps prevent overcrowding, because no significant reproduction occurs. The redear sunfish/green sunfish cross is another popular hybrid produced and stocked by some state fish hatcheries.

A disadvantage is that hybrids compete for habitat with wild sunfish. Also, they don't provide a significant food source for black bass and other predators, because they rarely bear young. For these reasons, they are only stocked in selective waters.

If the scrappy sunfish at the end of your line looks a little like this, a little like that, don't get excited. It's doubtful you've discovered a new, fights-like-the-dickens species of panfish; it's probably just a hybrid.

Catch a sackful and enjoy!

The spotted sunfish is an inhabitant of the South. Known also as stumpknocker, the fish can be found as far west as East Texas and as far north as southern Indiana and Ohio.

The Other Sunfish

Bluegills, as indicated in this display, stay around to guard the eggs and fry after spawning, making them vulnerable to a wide variety of jig lures.

Complete Angler's Library

More Sunnies

There are several other species of sunfish you may encounter during your panfishing junkets around the country. Some like the bantam sunfish, dollar sunfish and orange-spotted sunfish are fairly widespread, especially in the South, yet they seldom get as big as even a longear or pumpkinseed. A 3- to 4-incher is a leviathan, and these diminutive critters are usually too small to be of value as sportfish.

Others species have a much more limited distribution but may provide excellent sport in the few locations where they are found.

The Sacramento perch (Archoplites interruptus) is one such fish. Found in California, Nevada, Utah, Colorado and the Dakotas, this is the only sunfish native to the region west of the Rockies. It averages around a pound, with occasional individuals going over 3 pounds. It is quite popular within its limited range. The 4-pound, 9-ounce world record was caught in Pyramid Lake, Nevada, in 1971.

The flier (Centrarchus macropterus) is another member of the sunfish family occasionally encountered by anglers seeking other panfish. Though its range is quite expansive, taking in swamps, bayous and other weedy waters throughout much of the southeastern U.S., it is common nowhere, and only a few waters contain enough sizable fliers to provide quality fishing. The average size of this crappie-lookalike is only a few ounces, and though it accepts a variety of small baits and lures and is an excellent table fish, few anglers consider it worthy of their attention.

The Rio Grande perch (Cichlasoma cyanoguttatum) was originally restricted to the lower reaches of the Rio Grande drainage in Texas, but it was subsequently established in the Edwards Plateau region of central Texas in large warm-water springs. It is neither a perch nor a sunfish, but is mentioned here because it superficially resembles the sunfishes and deserves at least some recognition. In most waters, Rio Grande perch, or "guinea perch" as they're sometimes known, average around $1/2$ to $3/4$ pound, but they sometimes top the 2-pound mark. They fight long and hard, and are said to outclass black bass for strength and determination.

7

Finding And Catching Sunfish

N ow that you know something about the biology and
habits of America's sunfish, let's delve into methods
for finding and catching them. Using the right techniques under the right conditions, sunfish can be
caught year-round. The spawning season is one of the most productive fishing times. But sunfish can also provide exciting action
in early spring before the spawn and in late summer after the
spawn. The fun continues, right on through autumn and winter, a
fact that many northern ice fishermen know quite well.

Tackle Selection
Practically any type of fishing tackle can be applied to sunfish
angling, so long as the hook isn't too large. But anglers who consistently bring in lots of big sunnies almost invariably use the lightest
tackle practical.
Sunfish, especially big sunfish, tend to be rather cautious, and
the smashing, impulsive strikes typical of bass are seldom seen. A
sunfish usually swims up to a bait and spends a moment or two inspecting the offering before it strikes. Using fine line, inconspicu-
ous terminal tackle, and tiny baits or lures helps over come this
natural apprehension, while using light or ultra-light rods or poles
compounds the excitement of playing a fish.

Establishing A Fishing Pattern
Once you've selected the proper tackle, you must determine

The redear's premier quality is size, and this one may seem average when compared with many caught in Southern waters. However, a stringer of this size still results in a feast.

Finding And Catching Sunfish

where fish are, what baits and lures they will accept and what specific fishing techniques are most productive. In other words, you must establish a fishing pattern.

Sunfish feed at all levels, grubbing on the bottom, picking food from aquatic vegetation at mid-depths, and taking insects on the surface. They may be buried in dense cover, or they may be in relatively open water. Yellow jigs may be preferred one day, black the next. They may be biting only around dawn and dusk, or feeding heavily at night. Anglers must contend with these and other variables on every fishing trip they make.

Fortunately, if you go about your fish finding systematically, you shouldn't have much trouble determining where and how to fish, even when visiting new waters. To start, consider these factors when hitting the water.

First, consider time of day. Sunfish usually bite best in early morning and late afternoon. During rainy or cloudy days, midday fishing may be good, and if the fish are biting at all, there will almost always be some activity throughout the day. Still, peak activity is usually during the couple of hours right after sunrise and just before sunset, and if possible, you should plan your fishing time to coincide with these periods.

Habitat Preferences

All sunfish are cover lovers. Only rarely will they venture away from areas providing protection from predators, a ready supply of food, and shelter from intense sunlight. Concentrate your fishing in areas supplying these needs.

Search for bluegills, redears and other lake and pond dwellers around weedbeds, brushpiles, fallen or standing timber, boat docks, riprapped banks, stump fields and other cover. Stream-loving sunfish, like the redbreast, green sunfish, spotted sunfish and longear, are usually found in fairly deep pools out of the fast current, usually near some type of rocky or woody cover. They hide around boulders, fallen timber, root wads, weedbeds and undercut banks. But even the shade of an overhanging tree may help concentrate fish.

Other types of habitat preferences should also be considered. For instance, redear sunfish are primarily bottom feeders and are usually caught on or very near the bottom. Pumpkinseeds and redbreasts are occasionally caught on the surface or at mid-depth, but

Hitting shallow brush and weeds hard is a good way to string up a bunch of spawning redears. Since redears are primarily bottom-feeders, look for the non-spawners on or near the bottom.

they, too, are more susceptible to bottomfishing tactics. Adjust your fishing methods to suit the habits of the particular species of fish you seek.

Bait, Lure And Presentation Preferences

Seldom will any feeding sunfish ignore a properly presented offering of worms, crickets or tiny jigs. If these aren't producing, though, vary your offerings until you can establish a preference. Insect larvae like maggots, mealworms, catalpa worms, grubs and hellgrammites will be readily eaten by most sunfish. Grass shrimp, mussel meat and small crayfish are relished by redears, redbreasts and others. Several sunfish (greenies, longears and redbreasts in particular) will accept small minnows. Other excellent live baits include small leeches, grasshoppers, roaches and, for spotted sunfish and other tidal waters residents, small pieces of crab, shrimp or clams. Offbeat baits like bread balls, chicken liver and catfish stinkbait are also productive at times.

The selection of sunfish-catching artificials is no less extensive. Small jigs, spinners, lifelike plastics (i.e. plastic worms, plastic crickets and other imitations) and ultra-light plugs are among

Finding And Catching Sunfish

the best, but sunfish will also strike tiny spoons and a variety of fly fishing lures like wet and dry flies, nymphs and streamers.

Remember two key points about artificials. First, stick to smaller sizes. Most sunfish have tiny mouths, and even big-mouthed species like the green sunfish are more susceptible to small lures. Second, use lures resembling natural foods of the sunfish you are seeking. For instance, popping bugs work great for bluegills which feed on surface insects, but they aren't nearly as effective on bottom-feeding redears. Examining the stomach contents of the first sunfish you catch may help you home in on good lures and baits.

Be flexible in your presentations. If one thing doesn't work, try another. Change the color, size or style of lure you're using, vary the speed of your retrieve, experiment with different types of lures and baits, use lighter line. Sooner or later, if fish are biting at all, and you've come prepared with an assortment of tackle and baits, you should pinpoint a productive method.

One of the nicest things about sunfish is their propensity for feeding year-round. Seasonal fishing patterns may change considerably from one body of water to another, under various weather conditions, and in response to other physical factors like available cover and structure. But there are some basic facts you can use to help you locate and catch sunfish during each season.

The Spawning Spree

Several events during spawning time make this a "good luck" season for NAFC members seeking sunfish. First, during the week or two just prior to the actual spawn, sunfish go on a feeding frenzy to offset their reproductive growth spurt. They're also trying to add energy reserves for the stressful spawning season when activity increases. Sunfish are feeding more, so this is a great time to catch a real mess of fish.

Once male sunfish have established their nesting territory, they become much more aggressive and will make a big effort to keep all intruders—insects, worms, crayfish, minnows, whatever—away from the nest. Sunfish anglers can turn this aggression into a fishing boon, and many sunnies taken during this period take the bait not because it represents food, but because it has intruded into their nesting territory.

Another fact in the angler's favor is the concentration of fish during the spawn. There may be dozens of nests in a bedding area little bigger than a schoolbus, and there may be several beds this size along a 100-yard stretch of shoreline. Because sunfish are horded up in the shallows, they're simpler to find and should be that much easier to catch.

All this is pretty much common sense if you have a decent understanding of general sunfish spawning behavior. But there are several nuances of the spawn that may not be readily apparent until you've done further studying.

One is the fact that the largest sunfish—the big bulls and egg-laden females—will often be stationed in deeper water while small males prepare their nests. For this reason, you should work deeper sites out away from shallow-water beds. Big sunfish have been around long enough to be considerably more wary than their

Spawning Conditions For Sunfish

SPECIES	SPAWNING STARTS (AVG. WATER TEMP.)	PREFERRED BOTTOM TYPE	TYPICAL NESTING DEPTH
Bluegill	69° F	Sand or fine gravel	1 to 2½ ft.
Redear	68° F	Softer bottoms in water lillies	1½ to 3 ft.
Pumpkinseed	68° F	Sand or fine gravel	6 inches to 1½ ft.
Redbreast	68° F	Sand or fine gravel	6 inches to 1½ ft.
Warmouth	70° F	Small rock, lightly covered with silt	1½ to 4½ ft.
Green	71° F	Gravel	6 inches to 1 ft.
Longear	72° F	Gravel	6 inches to 1 ft.

Here in chart form is the average temperature, bottom-type preferred and water depth for spawning for seven major sunfish species from bluegills to longears.

smaller counterparts, and finding these angler-shy slabs may require fishing depths of 5 to 10 feet, something few anglers consider when so many nice fish are on bankside beds.

Another fact to remember is that spawning activity is spread out over a considerable period of time. Not all females are ripe at the same time, and individuals may deposit eggs in batches over two weeks or more. Sunfish may also spawn two or more times over the course of the spring and summer. These things assure at least some successful reproduction and provide anglers with outstanding shallow-water fishing for an extended period. You can visit the same beds time and time again during spring and summer and still catch fish.

To locate sunfish beds in clear-water lakes, you can often put on a pair of polarized sunglasses and roam the shorelines until you see clusters of white, plate-sized hollows that indicate a bedding area. Single nests are the norm for some species, but with most, there will usually be a dozen or more nests tightly grouped, with the rims almost touching.

In lakes with muddy or stained water, visual location of beds won't work. In these areas, try finding bottom substrate suitable for spawning. Odds are, you'll find spawning sunfish over sand, hard clay, gravel or shell bottom most of the time. With a little experience, you can probe the bottom with a long paddle or pole to locate such areas by feel and sound.

During calm days, bedding bream can sometimes be located by looking for patches of foam on the water's surface. If the wind's not blowing too hard, there will often be foamy bubbles that resemble soap suds floating on the water above the beds. If you have a keen nose, you may also be able to detect a fishy or oily smell in the air that can indicate bedding sunfish nearby.

Monitor water temperature to determine when to begin searching for bedding sunfish. Bluegills, redears and redbreasts usually spawn at temperatures of 67 to 70 degrees F. Typical spawning temperatures for other selected species are longear sunfish, 70-75 degrees; green sunfish, 69-73 degrees; and pumpkinseeds, 66-70 degrees.

After you've located a hot sunfish bed, remember it . . . forever. If you don't, some other angler will. Sunfish use the same spawning locations year after year so it will pay to make accurate notes of your location so you can return to the same spot next year.

This panfisherman is fishing a drop-off where panfish are holding. He was able to quickly locate this prime fish-catching structure with the use of a sonar flasher unit mounted on the boat.

Hot Weather Haunts And Hints

When summer's heat drives water temperatures to extremely high temperatures, sunfish are more likely to be feeding during low-light periods, coming into the shallows only at night or during early morning and late afternoon. Most will retreat to deep, well-oxygenated waters affording cool, shady cover. Among the best such areas for finding sunfish are in the shade of boat docks, bridges and green weedbeds.

•**Boat docks** are one of the first places you should head when seeking summer sunnies. But not just any ol' dock will do. The best are built on wood pilings, are in 5 to 15 feet of water near cover or structure, have been in the water several seasons, and lie very close to the water's surface. Docks meeting these criteria are extremely attractive to sunfish, because they provide prolonged shade throughout the day. The wood pilings provide a comfortable sense of security, which structure-oriented sunfish require, and also harbor a smorgasbord of foods. Moss growing on the seasoned wood may hide grass shrimp, newly hatched minnows, aquatic insects, insect larvae and other sunfish favorites. Plenty of yummy stuff falls *off* the dock, too, including spiders, roaches,

Finding And Catching Sunfish

crickets, moths and other flying and crawling insects. Size should be another consideration. Think of docks as fish hotels. Big hotels have rooms for lots of guests. Occupancy is limited, though, at smaller establishments. If other traits are equal, concentrate on large docks. Savvy anglers move in close and fish under the dock where big sunfish hide. A short, light spinning or spincasting outfit is handy for this kind of fishing, since it allows anglers to skip, flip and ricochet a bait or lure into even the tightest areas. Use slow-falling baits like lightweight twister-tail jigs or unweighted crickets to mimic falling insects. Flip these under the dock, and prepare for a strike as the bait falls. If a hit is not forthcoming, a slow retrieve close to the bottom will frequently produce.

•**Bridges** are also very attractive to hot-weather sunfish. The deep, shaded channel that usually runs underneath provides a constant supply of cool, aerated water, and the pilings are covered with algae which attracts aquatic invertebrates, small fish and other foods. First, fish around the pilings. You can use a sonar unit to help locate sunfish concentrations, or simply work various depths until fish are found. Throw a small jig, spinner or slightly weighted live bait past the piling, then let it drift down to feeding fish while you count. Once a fish is caught, count down to the same level on your next cast and catch another. Take care not to bump the pilings as this frightens fish away from the structure. After fishing the pilings, be sure to work the rock riprap that usually lines the shore under bridges. Cast parallel to the shore, starting fairly deep and gradually working deeper as you move away from the bank. Deep-diving, ultra-light, crayfish-imitation crankbaits are a real killer in these waters.

•**Weedbeds** can also provide exciting summer action for those who know how to penetrate the mess. Most anglers assume that since they can't see open water, the area can't be fished, and they go about angling in the usual way of pecking along the edges. But sunfish, especially the heavyweight elders, are deep within the greenery. The trick to catching these slabs is working methodically to cover every accessible nook and pocket. A cane pole or jigging pole is tops for this, because it allows you to reach likely honeyholes from a distance with fewer hang-ups. Attach a bobber above your bait—jigs, crickets, grass shrimp and worms are good choices—and probe every opening you see, changing the position of the bobber occasionally until you determine the depth where

Boat docks are one of the first places anglers should search for hot-weather sunnies. Lots of shade and a ready food supply around the dock supports attract lots of sunfish.

Finding And Catching Sunfish

fish are feeding at that particular time.

Don't be shy about fishing tiny, "impossible" looking openings. Chances are, your bait will penetrate quite easily, and sunfish in these particular places are far more likely to strike than those found along an edge that has been pounded by anglers in every passing boat.

Autumn And Winter Angling

Once summer has passed, many sunfish anglers store away their fishing equipment until spring spawning season rolls around again. Interest wanes, because most fishermen believe feeding activity has all but ceased.

Fortunately, the facts don't jibe with that belief. Not only can sunfish be caught during autumn and winter, these are excellent times to boat a mess. Some sunfish continue feeding all winter, and species like the bluegill are prime targets of most all winter ice fishermen.

Autumn brings cooler water temperatures, and as fall turnover begins, sunfish in lakes and ponds scatter, with concentrations difficult to pinpoint. Some will be shallow, others deep, and the angler may have to stay on the move to pick up numbers of fish. Trolling and drift fishing are good methods for locating fall sunfish, but if that fails, leapfrog through shallow-water cover areas. Try your pet baits around docks, piers, lily pads, reeds, cattails, brushy shorelines, over ridges and reefs, in old creek channels and where waters deepen over rocky and weedy points.

Stream fishing is really outstanding in autumn. These flowing environments aren't subject to the vagaries of turnover, so sunfish may be found in familiar haunts. To catch them, rig a live bait tidbit or small jig beneath a bobber, and float it past boulders, fallen timber, sharply sloping gravel bars, underwater ledges, creek mouths, undercut banks on outside bends and other types of cover and structure.

As winter arrives, and the water cools even more, sunfish move back to the same deep-water haunts used in summer, and can be caught using many summer tactics. Later in the season, as the water temperature begins creeping back upward, a burgeoning hunger brought on by winter's period of near starvation stimulates an increase in feeding activity. Inlet streams where incoming water is warmer than the lake or river can be hotspots at this time.

Complete Angler's Library

Just prior to the spawn, look for sunfish along prominent underwater structure that leads from deep water to the shallows—features like underwater stream channels, long sloping points and dropoffs along shallow flats.

Catching winter sunfish is challenging, to say the least. If the water temperature falls extremely low, they become very lethargic and may quit feeding altogether. Those that are feeding may bite so gingerly they are almost undetectable.

To overcome these problems, try fishing directly on, or just inches above, the bottom, as that's where winter fish are likely to be; using live baits or artificials resembling nymphs and aquatic worms that are usually abundant in bottom mud or gravel where sunfish stay; keeping your baits as small as possible for, in cold water, sunfish may nudge but not seize larger baits, yet gently nibble and take small ones; and, moving your bait very slowly, if at all, and watching your line constantly for any slight movement.

Regardless of the season, the key to finding and catching sunfish is flexibility. Once you do establish a productive pattern, tuck it away in your memory for future reference. Chances are good the same fishing pattern will bring you success again.

8

Catching Sunfish In Special Situations

Whether you're a swimmer, water-skier or diver, you're probably thrilled when you can enjoy your pastime in a sparkling clear body of water. If you enjoy fishing, too, however, you also know clear water can be a despicable spoiler of angling fun. Clear water is the angler's bane, and unless you know how to overcome problems it presents, you can face many fishless hours.

Fishing ultra-clear waters presents special challenges for the sunfish angler. Sunfish in such a visible environment are especially cautious and respond differently to most factors than sunfish living in stained or muddy water. Their world is under a magnifying glass, and they know it. Mistakes or miscalculations are not easily forgiven in clear waters.

Clear waters may be found in ponds, streams, lakes, bayous or quarries. Many are drinking-water clear year-round; others clear up only during the low-rainfall periods of summer and winter. Spring rains and runoff, as well as the turbulence of fall turnover, tend to discolor the water during those times, but in between, the water becomes virtually or entirely transparent. Unfortunately, it's during these "in between" times that sunfish become more difficult to catch, even without the additional hindrance of ultra-clear waters.

Catching Sunfish In Ultra-Clear Waters

Clear water has several major effects on sunfish behavior, loca-

A johnboat is the perfect craft, because of its shallow draft, for fishing shallow, timber-infested lakes like this Arkansas oxbow which would be off-limits to deeper hull boats.

Catching Sunfish In Special Situations

tion and feeding strategies. To better understand those effects, let's use a weather analogy.

Clear water is like a cloudless, sunny day when visibility is almost totally unrestricted. Under this condition, sunfish rely heavily on sight to find their prey. They can see your offerings well so they often are more discriminating. Light penetration is good, so weeds grow deeper, and oxygen is found farther down. Consequently, sunfish will often be deeper as well.

Sunfish in clear water tend to shy away from bright sunlight, favoring darker waters for ambushing food and hiding from predators. They feed more around dawn and dusk. Feeding at night is common, and fish will be more active on cloudy, overcast days. Sunfish will also tend to roam more in clear waters and are more easily spooked by careless anglers.

When seeking sunfish in clear water, the careful, quiet approach is usually most productive. Movements should be slow and deliberate. Plan your boating route to take advantage of shoreline cover for camouflage. Wearing shades of light blue or gray helps you blend with the sky. Only your bait, not you, should be seen by the sunfish.

Fishing during limited light periods is the key to success on many clear waters. In early morning and late afternoon, light penetration is minimal, and fish may move into forage-filled shallows to feed. Cloudy days can be good for many hours of successful clear-water sunfishing, and during the heat of summer, many sunfish fans enjoy night-fishing. During low-light periods, you also minimize the problem of spooking fish before you can hook one.

It's usually difficult to catch sunfish in clear water when fishing too close to the fish's haunts. Long casts are important, so it's best to forget the cane poles and jigging poles, and fish with an ultralight spinning or spincast outfit capable of tossing the lightest lure several yards.

Using light line helps gain extra yardage on your casts. It's also an effective way to entice more strikes from finicky sunfish. The diameter of light line is smaller, so the line is more difficult for fish to detect. Less line resistance means lures will run deeper as well.

The habitat being fished is a definite consideration in determining the line size to use in clear waters. Where cover is dense, 8-pound line may be as light as you dare go. But on a deep, cover-barren reservoir, the choice might be 4-, 2- or even 1-pound test

Double Anchoring Over a School

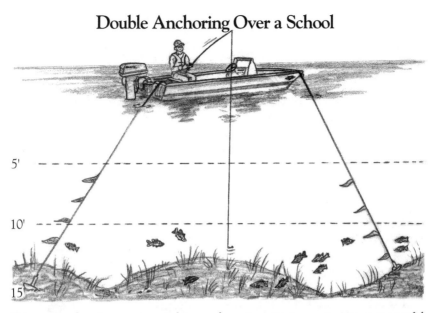

5'

10'

15'

Using two anchors in current or wind is a good way to maintain your position over a panfish school. After locating the school, throw out a marker buoy and anchor at that spot.

for best action. You may also want to use clear or low-visibility line to give you an edge, particularly during bright days. Line considerations are extremely important in a crystal-clear environment where sunfish look closely at the prey before attacking.

Choosing Lures For Clear Water

Lures are another important consideration under clear-water conditions. When presented naturally, live baits are by far the best choice in transparent waters; there's nothing phony for sunfish to observe. If you prefer using jigs, spinners or other artificials, though, stick to the smaller versions. A $^1/_{48}$-ounce jig may out-produce a $^1/_{32}$-ounce jig in clear water, and likewise, a $^1/_{64}$-ounce jig will probably work better than a $^1/_{48}$-ounce jig. Terminal tackle like swivels and sinkers should be avoided altogether if possible.

Lures can be retrieved faster in clear waters, often triggering impulse strikes. If sunfish appear aggressive, use a rapid retrieve and active bait. A jig/spinner combination will often draw a response from a bluegill or redbreast several feet away. Natural-looking artificials that resemble tiny crayfish, shad, worms, grubs or other forage can also be effective. Chartreuse, white and other light-colored lures seem to be productive for the majority of clear-water jig fishermen.

Catching Sunfish In Ponds

Ponds offer excellent fishing for a variety of sunfish. Bluegills, redears and green sunfish adapt especially well to the small pond ecosystem, and in some areas, ponds may also have pumpkinseeds, redbreast sunfish, longears or other sunnies.

Many sunfish anglers shy away from ponds because they believe these diminutive waters aren't big enough to support good numbers of good-sized fish. But if you examine state-record listings published by the National Fresh Water Fishing Hall of Fame, you'll quickly discover that idea doesn't hold water. Of 47 state-record bluegills listed, 23 (49 percent) were caught in ponds, including seven over 3 pounds and 12 between 2 and 3 pounds. Thirteen (52 percent) of the 25 state-record redear sunfish listed came from ponds, including three over 4 pounds, six between 3 and 4 pounds, and two between 2 and 3 pounds. Ponds also accounted for 50 percent of the state-record green sunfish, 50 percent of the state-record longears, and 29 percent of the state-record pumpkinseeds. Some poorly managed ponds are inhabited by tiny, stunted sunfish, but those with balanced populations of predator and prey fish can provide fast-paced fishing for heavyweight sunfish.

Though pond fishing exemplifies sunfish angling at its simplest and best, there's more to catching pond fish than just wetting a hook. Identifying the correct techniques, presentation, baits and locational factors is important even on these small waters.

Simply put, a pond is smaller than a lake, ranging from $1/2$ acre to perhaps 25 acres in size. Ponds which can be man-made usually have such things as structure, vegetation and water clarity that can provide keys to catching fish. Pond water may come from runoff, and underground springs or a feeder creek whose channel may be covered by the pond. Some are clear, others are muddy. Most ponds are also shallow so you can probe virtually every level.

Spawning season action starts sooner, because the shallow pond water warms more quickly than in large lakes. During this period, one simple method of fishing is to rig up a pole with a small, long-shanked hook, light line, a split shot or two, and a fixed bobber set at a shallow depth. Use worms or crickets for bait, and, walking the banks, look for fish congregated on their beds in

The best panfish baits for any given situation will vary from water to water. This angler caught this bluegill in a stream pool on an often overlooked bait—a small frog.

shallow, sheltered water. Polarized sunglasses are a big help here, enabling you to better spot the dish-shaped nests and also helping you detect various forms of cover or changes in bottom makeup (rocks, gravel, weeds, logs, obstructions) that cause fish to congregate in those spots.

Tips For Pond Action

Once a bedding area is located, use your long pole to quietly deposit your bait within the area. You should also fish beyond the visible beds, in slightly deeper water. That's where large fish will often be stationed, especially just before and after spawning.

Pond sunfish may be found near shoreline cover and structure not only during spawning season, but throughout the warm months and into autumn. During periods of temperature extremes, though, especially during mid-summer and winter, they frequent the deepest water providing adequate oxygen. Often, they lay right on the bottom, and given a choice, they will be near some type of cover or structure. A deep-water area containing an isolated snag is preferred by the fish over deep water with no such object, for example.

Fishing directly on the bottom is a good tactic for nabbing hot and cold weather fish, using either live bait or mini-jigs. Small spinners, wet flies and miniature deep-diving crankbaits can also be effective when fished slowly over the substrate.

If fishing is slow, try using the "fan" system to locate sunfish. Begin casting to your left, working your bait along the shore. Move in a clockwise direction, placing each successive cast three feet (or even less) from the previous cast and continuing in a broad arc. Use whatever number of casts it takes to reach the shoreline to your right. Then, if you still haven't found fish, move down the shore and start again, covering a new plot of water.

This method helps you cover the pond in a most thorough fashion, but you must also remember to cover all depths. How?

Nearly all man-made ponds have a dam or levee at one end, and we know that water is usually deeper near the dam. Let's start there and try to determine at what depth fish are located. This is done through several series of fan casts fished at different depths, starting at one corner of the dam.

On the first series of casts, the bait or lure is retrieved at a shallow depth. The second series should be mid-depth retrieves, and the third series should be along the floor of the pond. Change lures or bobber position if necessary to achieve the desired depth. At whatever depth you find fish is obviously the depth at which you should continue fishing.

Creek coves, where feeder creeks enter a pond, are good places during spring and early autumn when sunfish are ready to invade the shallows. In-flowing creek water also provides relief from extreme summer and winter temperatures. Water coming into the pond is usually much cooler or warmer than the pond itself.

Look for sunfish hanging right on the edge of the creek channel. The channel usually runs through the cove and passes somewhere through the mouth of the cove. For thorough coverage, fish both sides of the cove mouth carefully, trying to locate sunfish holding along the dropoff the channel creates. Then move back

Want to put even more fun into catching these scrappy sunfish? The answer is to use ultralight gear and tackle, paired with light test-weight line, for some real battles.

into the cove and fish the spot where the creek enters the pond by fanning a series of casts to cover the entire area.

Pay Attention To Cover

Vegetation should also get your attention in ponds. Plant cover not only provides food, comfort and safety for sunfish, it can also indicate the bottom structure of the pond. For instance, weed growth commencing along the shoreline and extending out 30 or 40 feet indicates a shallow flat. The bottom may drop sharply where the weedline ends, something you should check out.

Look for small islands of weeds separate from the distinct contour of the shoreline, as these are exceptional sunfish attractors. Usually, one side will contain deeper water than the other. This is the place to fish, but be sure to work your bait as close to the weedline as possible.

Look, too, for openings in the weedbeds where you can drop in a bait or lure. Sunfish love these cool, food-rich confines, and any natural looking offering presented here is likely to be devoured. Any changes in contour (pockets or indentations) along the edge of the weeds should also be investigated.

In sizing up a pond, also look for rock piles, stickups, stumps, logs, trees, holes, humps and points. These are typical sunfish hotspots and should be fished thoroughly. Any brush or sub-merged objects offshore deserve special attention, as do docks and piers, deep holes around in-flowing water pumps, cool spots beneath overhanging trees, and riprap along shore.

Ponds may not look like much, but they offer superb sunfishing opportunities far out of proportion to their size. If you're a devoted sunfish fan, visit these bantam waters as often as possible. No other type of water offers such excellent fishing in such a small area. Ponds are easy to find, easy to learn and easy to fish. They're also easy to fall in love with.

So find a pond, learn it, fish it and love it. The dividends you reap will far exceed your considerable investment in time, equipment and effort.

Taking Sunfish In Deep Water

Taking big sunfish consistently from shallow-water haunts is easy. But when extremes of summer heat or winter cold drive them down into deeper water, catching them can be difficult and requires special fishing techniques.

To master deep-water fishing, you should first understand why fish move to deep water. To do that, think of a lake or pond as a triple-decker sandwich cookie—two thick layers of cookie with a thinner layer of cream filling between them. In summer, many lakes and ponds stratify into three layers, with the warmest, oxygen-rich water on top, cold oxygen-free water on bottom, and a middle layer of cool, oxygen-rich water called the thermocline in between. The thermocline, like the filling in the cookie, is the best part, because that's where deep-water sunfish are likely to concentrate. Of the three layers, this one usually best satisfies the sunfish's needs for dissolved oxygen and water temperature.

The depth and thickness of the thermocline will vary from one body of water to another. In some ponds, it may be five feet down and only a foot thick; in extremely large, deep lakes, it may be 20 feet down and several feet thick. Regardless of its location and size, though, the thermocline is where nearly all sizable sunfish will be during periods of temperature extremes. And though the thermocline doesn't occupy the deepest part of the lake or pond, it's still far deeper than the thin layer of surface water most sunfish anglers usually fish.

To locate deep-water sunfish, first locate the thermocline.

Sunfish love to frequent dense woody cover found in and around beaver lodges. Working a jig in and around these structures is a good way to catch sunnies with little effort. Anglers often use heavier line because of the inevitable snags.

This is relatively simple. Lower a thermometer into the water and take temperature readings at various depths. The temperature will probably change very little the first several feet, but at some point—usually between 5 to 20 feet deep—the temperature will drop quickly, falling 5 to 10 degrees within a fairly short distance. *Voila!* You have found the thermocline, and this is the depth you should fish.

Okay, so now you've identified the band of water where deep-water sunfish are likely to be. What next? A depth sounder will help you locate cover or structure where sunfish might concentrate—a channel dropoff, an underwater hump, the edge of an inundated pond or perhaps a cluster of tall stumps beneath the surface. If you don't have a depth sounder, look for topside features that appear to continue underwater to the desired depth—bridge or dock pilings, long steeply sloping points, rocky ledges, toppled trees or the outside edge of a weedbed.

Once you've found such areas, you're ready to fish. And when fishing deep water, nothing can beat an ultra-light rod and a tiny reel filled with 2- or 4-pound test line. This rig exhibits sensitivity not found with larger tackle and permits you to detect the most delicate nibbles. It also turns every fish you hook into a whopper. Fighting a $^3/_4$-pound bluegill up out of 15 feet of water on 2-pound line and a mere switch of a rod isn't as easy as it sounds.

A tightline live bait set-up is the best choice for taking bottom-feeding sunfish in areas where the thermocline touches the lakebed. Thread a slip sinker on your line, and, below it, tie on a barrel swivel just large enough to keep the sinker from sliding off. To the swivel's lower eye, tie a 2- or 3-foot leader of light line tipped with a small, light-wire hook. Add your favorite live bait—worms, crickets and larvae baits are excellent choices—then cast the rig out and allow it to settle to the bottom. When a sunfish takes the bait, the line moves freely through the sinker with no resistance to alert fish to a possible threat.

If fish seem persnickety, do away with the sinker altogether. Without any weight except that of the hook, a cricket or worm sinks very, very slowly, providing almost irresistible allure to down-under sunnies. As the bait sinks, watch the line very closely for any slight movement indicating a hit.

Fly rod anglers can also score heavily on deep-water sunfish. Wet flies resembling insect larvae and nymphs are especially effective. A sinking fly line can carry these patterns down where big sunfish are feeding and produce pleasing results. Work the flies in short hops. The sight of such a fidgety tidbit is certain to tempt even the most jaded piscatorial taste buds.

If sunfish are suspended, try fishing a small jig under a bobber. If they aren't deeper than the length of your rod or pole, you can merely clamp a plastic bobber on your line, and dangle the jig below it at the proper depth. When you cast, the jig sinks to the right depth and stays there while you retrieve it with twitches that lend a lifelike action.

If sunfish are deeper than your rod is long, rig a sliding bobber above the jig to make casting easier. To do this, tie a short piece of rubber band around your line at the depth you want to fish. When the bobber hits the water, the weight of the jig pulls line through the bobber until the rubber band abuts the float. Your jig is automatically at the depth you selected, and you can easily adjust the depth by moving the rubber up or down the line. The knot will easily pass through your line guides and wind onto the reel spool. It's simple and effective.

If you're tired of catching scrawny little sunfish, search out the depths during summer and winter. That's where the big ones will usually be. Deep-water fishing fills what might otherwise be an empty spot on your fishing itinerary, and that's worth fishing in the heat and the cold.

Catching Sunfish In Streams

The word "stream" can describe practically any body of flowing water, from a tiny creek to a river the size of the Mississippi. Here, though, we'll concentrate on streams small enough you'd have no trouble tossing a pebble from one side to the other. Small streams are found throughout the country, sometimes several to the mile, and each may be home to several species of sunfish, including redbreasts, longears, bluegills, green sunfish, spotted sunfish and others.

Fishing for small-stream sunnies is like hunting with a rod. Many creatures would eagerly devour these fish, so they are a nervous and wary lot, ready to streak for cover at the slightest intrusion. The silhouette of a standing angler will send them under rocks, brushpiles and cutbanks in short order. So, like a hunter, you must slip up on the prey unannounced and do your work with extreme stealth.

Any decent cover in a foot or more of water is a potential sunfish hideout. Cast upstream or quartering upstream to fallen trees, boulders, brushpiles and ledges adjacent to deep water; along the edges of coontail, willow shoots and other vegetation; under overhangs, rootwads and logs along the banks; and any place where the water drops into a pool or run. The best of these spots will be in or near long, deep pools, so when you encounter a big hole or long stretch of deeper water, work it methodically. Drop successive casts about a foot apart, covering a number of different depths until fish are found.

One technique that elicits smashing strikes is to cast up on the rocks or the bank and jump the bait or lure into the water. Sunfish get a bit crazy when a popping bug or cricket behaves in this man-

Sunfish can find a home in just about any type of water so long as it's not too polluted. Fishing these small creeks from the bank can produce an assortment of battling panfish.

ner, or when a tiny spinner leaps from the bank and starts swimming away.

Any bait or lure you use elsewhere will work here as well, but the best bait might be right under your feet. Tiny crayfish, nymphs, scuds, leeches and insect larvae can often be found under rocks in the stream. Worms can sometimes be found in leaf litter along the shore. Impaled on a small hook and drifted through a deep hole, these baits can entice a hefty sunfish when your pet artificials aren't producing.

When stream fishing, remember these additional guidelines that will lead you to bigger catches of sunfish. Fish upstream whenever possible. When walking the shore, always fish from the shallow side, entering the water only when necessary. Should you enter the water, do so below the hole you plan to fish, so the moving current will carry your vibrations away from the fish. Stay as far back from the bank as cover will allow. Move quietly. Use small baits and lures and the lightest line feasible for the type of cover you're fishing.

Though you'll be able to fish most small streams by wading or walking the banks, a canoe or other boat can be much more productive than going afoot. You'll cover more territory and be able to fish locations inaccessible by wading. Belly boats or float tubes are useful for covering short stretches. And for a special taste of sunfishing fun, try a combined overnight campout and fishing expedition. Pan-fried sunfish never smell or taste better than they do when cooked over a streamside fire.

Crappies

9

Meet The Crappie

Fishermen enjoy catching two crappie species, the black and the white. Found exclusively in North America, crappies are native from south-central Canada to Texas and eastward, but they've been introduced throughout much of the West, too. The black crappie, found in a slightly wider range than the white, is the dominant species along the United States' northern tier, in southern Canada, Florida, and in the brackish water along the coasts. Both black and white crappies live in America's interior. In these regions' waters, white crappies often dominate, and whites are the main crappie species in some areas of Mexico.

The two species look somewhat alike; they're somewhat flat fish with rather long heads and in-turned foreheads. However, black crappies are a bit stockier than whites.

Black crappies are also generally darker. (Whites are commonly mistaken for blacks when the spawning male whites turn dark.) Both crappies have silvery sides and darker backs featuring tinges of green, purple or other colors. This countershading—dark top, light bottom—makes crappies less visible to predators and prey. The black crappie's irregular spots on its sides also camouflage it in certain weeds, gravel and similar cover. The spots are arranged in no particular pattern—a characteristic that helps you distinguish them from white crappies, which have blotches in vertical bands. The white's bands may help it hide within vertical-type cover—brush, weed stems and so on.

This slab crappie went for a jig and plastic tail. Crappies this size and larger don't swim in all crappie waters, but they can be found with regularity across most of the crappie's range.

Black Crappie

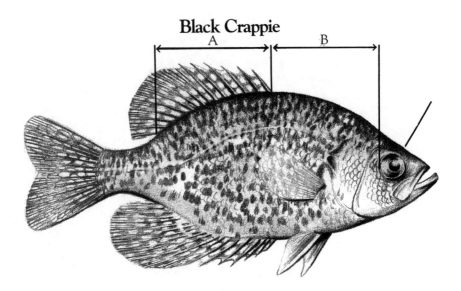

The black crappie has seven or eight hard dorsal spines. The length of the base of the dorsal fin (A) is about equal to the distance from the first spine to the eye (B). The head is not dished.

Another identification characteristic is that on the black crappie, the dorsal fin base approximately equals the distance from the black's dorsal to the eye. The white's dorsal base is shorter than the dorsal-to-eye length. Also, there are usually six spines in the white's dorsal fin, while the black's dorsal may sport six to 10 fin spines, though usually seven or eight. The crappie's scientific name, *Pomoxis*, means opercle sharp, referring to the pointed gill cover.

The Black Crappie

The black crappie (*Pomoxis nigromaculatus*) is known by numerous regional names, including strawberry bass, calico, calico bass, speckled perch, speck and sac-a-lait. A typical black crappie in many areas weighs $1/2$ pound with larger ones commonly exceeding a pound or two. The largest crappie ever officially weighed was a black crappie, and it weighed 6 pounds. A California study showed a five-year maximum age in two lakes tested, though in some waters most crappies may live just two or three years. Occasionally, an individual lives 10 years or more. Black crappies commonly inhabit clear, cool water in lakes, reservoirs,

White Crappie

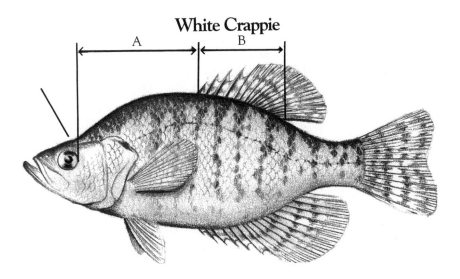

The white crappie has five or six hard dorsal spines. The length of the base of the dorsal fin (B) is always less than the distance from the first spine to the eye (A). The head is dished.

large ponds and large and medium-sized streams.

The species may grow fastest in large, clear reservoirs, slowest in turbid lakes. However, blacks thrive quite well in some murky waters. Blacks also tend to be found in acidic water (a pH of less than seven), as opposed to the whites favoring a pH of more than seven. Black crappies are also found in the brackish water along the coasts, more so than are white crappies. In a Louisiana study, the maximum salinity in waters where blacks were found was 2 parts per thousand.

Black crappies appeared to prefer water temperatures in the mid-70s to mid-80s in one study. Jeff Boxrucker, an Oklahoma fisheries research biologist, notes crappies, however, avoid excessively high temperatures, such as when a warm-water discharge at a power plant heats an area of a lake.

The Schooling Instinct

Black crappies don't "school" like shad or similar species; however, they roam in groups commonly known as schools. Black crappies might be found on a lake bottom, resting or food-hunting, but the species is noted for its habit of suspending—hovering or following forage, often swimming shallower than white crappies in the same water. Their travels may take them along weedbed edges, drop-off edges, around submerged timber and into the cover itself because that's where their food is.

Even when the fish are basically resting, opportunistic black crappie may nab a food item that comes by. The species, whether in Manitoba or Texas, eats insects, zooplankton, small crayfish and fish such as minnows and tiny rough and gamefish. Diet, however, varies with what's available in each water, and the season. Frequently, black crappies consume large numbers of insects and plankton in spring, fish in summer, larger baitfish and crayfish in fall, and insects and fish in winter.

Research shows murky-water blacks don't feed as efficiently as white crappies on forage like shad, so the blacks may feed on other items. And though you often catch black crappies and bluegills at the same spots, one Minnesota study notes these two species may feed at different levels at times, thus not competing for food.

Black crappies commonly feed heavily at night, and one study indicated blacks feed more at dusk than at dawn, and the least during daytime. Net catches also show blacks more active at dusk and at night than whites. However, seasonal food and water temperature changes can alter feeding times.

Spawning Blacks

Once black crappies are at least two or three years old, they spawn in the springtime. Blacks nest earlier in the spring overall than whites. In one study, spawning was noted in water as cold as 40 degrees but spawning generally takes place in the 60s and low 70s, with day length being an influence. Spawning may occur as early as February in Florida or as late as July in the Dakotas and Minnesota. Florida black crappies may also spawn in autumn.

Several males in a colony move to a suitable spawning ground and they sweep out several inch-wide nests—as many as 30 or more in 10 square feet. Later, females arrive to lay eggs and then leave for deeper water. Females may return to lay eggs several times before the spawn ends.

The spawning ground in very clear water may lie as deep as around 25 feet. In stained water, the nests are much shallower. However, even in clear water, blacks may nest just a few feet deep if heavy cover is present, such as thick reed beds. Black crappies

Sometimes it's difficult to tell the difference between a white and black crappie because the males of both species turn dark after spawning. This happens to be a male black crappie.

spawn on various bottoms including sand and muck, but the fish appear to favor bottoms associated with cover like brush and weeds. In streams, many crappies migrate upstream where they might end up below a dam and they spawn where the only cover available is riprap. Spawning causes diet changes. An Arizona study conducted at Roosevelt Lake, a large reservoir, showed threadfin shad was the normal fare year-round. But, during spawning, the males ate mostly plankton, the main food available near the nests. The females, though, ate a lot more shad because they were away from the nests more.

Crappies produce a high number of eggs per body weight compared to other Centrarchid species. After an Oklahoma lake was treated, only about 27 black crappies and 23 white crappies remained. A year later, their offspring were estimated at 136,000 black and 64,000 white. Crappies tend to overpopulate and become stunted in small ponds; however, biologists note black crappies don't overpopulate as much as whites. Black crappies can suffer from over-fishing.

Crappie eggs normally hatch out in a few days, but may take up to two weeks during cold weather. Males guard the tiny crappies until they're big enough to swim away and begin feeding on plankton. Year-old fish commonly reach 2 to 4 inches in length.

Black Crappie Senses

The black crappies' large eyes suggest they can see well, and they are sight feeders, especially in clearer waters. Eyes are set high on the head enabling them to effectively see and eat minnows above them. However, crappies are capable of catching small crayfish and insects crawling on the bottom, too. Crappies can see rather well both in daylight and, after eyes adjust, at night.

Crappies have a good sense of smell. Like other fish, they have nostrils leading to an olfactory organ, and they have four nostrils rather than two as in some species. Crappies also have taste buds. Finding food through taste and smell isn't as important as it is with catfish, but you can still observe crappies following or bumping the tails of baitfish or artificial lures, apparently testing them through reception of chemical stimuli.

Crappies can also hear well. They react to boat noises, and some anglers even claim to attract crappies by swishing a fishing rod in the water. Like other fish, a crappie's ears lay behind the eyes. Crappies also have the close-range sound-gathering organ, the lateral line, extending along the sides from head to tail.

Record Black Crappies

The world record black crappie, according to the National Fresh Water Fishing Hall of Fame, is a 6-pound fish caught by Lettie Robertson in the Westwego Canal, Louisiana, a Mississippi River backwater in 1969. That fish also is the largest black crappie caught on pole and line as Robertson used no reel.

The International Game Fish Association (IGFA), with different record requirements, lists L. Carl Herring Jr.'s 4-pound, 8-ounce fish as the world record. Herring caught it in Kerr Lake in Virginia in 1981.

World line class records include Herring's fish plus 4-pound,

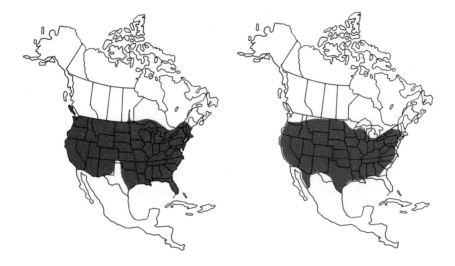

Both black (left map) and white crappies are generally found throughout the United States as indicated by these range maps. However, the black crappie tends to be more widespread.

4-ounce fish from Arkansas and Alabama. Fly fishing records include a 2-pound, 6-ounce Virginia black, and recent ice fishing records include a 3-pound, 8-ounce black crappie from Minnesota.

The average state record black crappie runs a little more than 3 1/2 pounds, and about 18 states have grown fish 4 pounds or heavier. Louisiana, with the world record fish, doesn't separate the two species in their records. Two states specifically list blacks of 5 pounds or more—Minnesota and South Carolina. Other top states known for giant black crappies have included Arizona, Kansas, Oklahoma, Arkansas, Ohio, Illinois, Missouri, Washington and Alabama.

A notable state record in the recent past was Alabama's 4-pound, 4-ounce black crappie, taken in 1984. The oldest record is Minnesota's, caught back in 1940. Another tough-to-beat record has been Michigan's 4-pound, 2-ounce fish caught in 1947. Two-thirds of the record black crappies were caught in lakes as opposed to ponds and streams.

The White Crappie

The popular white crappie is the sole crappie species in many waters and is commonly "king crappie" in waters harboring both species. White crappie waters now extend from nearly coast to coast, and from around North Dakota southward to well into Mexico. The species (*Pomoxis annularis*) is known by regional names such as silver perch, white perch, barfish, ringed crappie and bachelor shad. And though the white usually weighs less than a pound, it may reach 2 or more. The world record weighed 5 pounds, 3 ounces.

Research shows the white crappie tends to out-thrive the black when both are found in murky reservoirs, lakes, bayous, ox-bows and rivers. It's the main crappie species in many of our fa-mous, stained-water crappie reservoirs like Kentucky Lake.

However, even when both species live in clear water, the white again may dominate. One fisheries biologist notes black crappies supposedly do better in such waters, "but there are gener-ally more white crappie than black." Reservoirs' water levels fre-quently fluctuate which may affect the black crappie's spawn more than the white's.

Though a Northern lake black crappie may live longer, a white crappie in the South grows faster. An Oklahoma study showed white crappies grew faster in ponds and small lakes than in large lakes. Though they can grow older, of nearly a thousand white crappies tested at Kentucky Lake, none were over five years old. Many whites live only three or four years.

White Crappie Habitat

Whites live in both clear and turbid waters, and like blacks, swim shallower as turbidity increases. Unlike blacks, whites are more often found in water with a pH of more than seven.

According to a Lake Texoma sampling, no white crappies were found in water with less than 3.3 ppm oxygen. In Missouri's Lake of Ozarks, white crappies were found from zero to about 28 feet deep in early summer. In mid-summer, when crappies are thought to go deeper, they were seldom below 12 feet—because of low oxygen levels in deeper water. In September, they again could move down as oxygen conditions improved.

At Texoma, big white crappies were found to swim deeper than the small crappies, but small ones were more often captured in open water than along shore while the opposite was true of the large fish. The fish were evenly distributed in fall, near bottom in

The white crappie (above) is said to be more tolerant of murky waters and fluctuating water levels than the black. However, black crappies do quite well in some off-colored waters.

winter (about 26 feet), shallowest (about 17 feet) in spring, and somewhat deeper during the summer months.

White Crappie Foods

White crappies, like blacks, swim mainly where the food is. Catches in Oklahoma biologists' gillnets were best near concentrations of mayflies and small gizzard shad, both major foods.

But, as with black crappies, the diet may change seasonally. Whites over 12 inches, according to Kansas research at one lake, ate mostly fish but also insects and crayfish in April and May. In June, they ate mostly mayflies, and in July, mostly fish and some crayfish. In September-October the diet was all fish. In Texoma, shad and other fish were important June through January. Insects and plankton were consumed more during February through May.

Meet The Crappie

Like blacks, whites "school" while feeding and at rest, they can be opportunistic, and they may roam for food, though usually not great distances.

Generally, whites are more active March through October; whites feed less below 50 degrees. A Texas study showed that during summer white crappies fed all night, but in other seasons mostly at dawn and dusk. Illinois research pointed out that whites feed a lot more than blacks in daytime.

White Crappie Spawning

White crappies living in the same water as black crappies generally start nesting a little later than blacks and continue spawning later into summer. Spawning might occur at 57 to 73 degrees but often at 60 to 68 degrees. However, day length may play a more important role.

Whites spawn in protected areas on various materials, with colonies of males fanning away nests, three to four feet apart. One study suggested white crappies are more secretive than blacks, spawning a bit deeper, but occasionally black and white crappies crossbreed. White crappies may spawn shallower in cool years than when waters are warmer.

Spawn-time males, and occasionally females, turn dark for about six weeks. The polygamous female, one study showed, produces about 2,000 eggs (young females) to about 325,000 eggs (13-inch fish.) To curb crowding in some lakes such as Tennessee's Reelfoot, crappies have been commercially netted.

White crappie eggs under favorable conditions hatch in two to four days. The larvae measure about $1/16$ inch, a bit longer than black crappies. Larvae stay at the nest a few days, until about $1/8$ inch long. When 2 inches, or so they may go into deeper water.

Diet quality, more than quantity, affects the growth rate of young crappies. White crappies, age one, are commonly 2 to 4 inches. Spawning-age fish, two or three years old, are commonly 6 to 10 inches or more.

Besides food, white crappies may also need cover to grow best. Continuously drawn-down water (and the resulting cover loss) has caused poor growth. And in river oxbows, growth is better in those open to the river than in those separated, probably because of competition for limited food sources in the separated oxbows. White crappies in new reservoirs also generally grow faster than those in old reservoirs—in one case two-year-old crappies measured about 9 1/2 inches in a new reservoir compared to 5 inches for crappies the same age in an older reservoir.

The white crappie smells, tastes, hears and sees rather well, similar to the black crappie. However, one or more senses may be more developed in whites. It's not completely understood by biologists, but, despite low visibility in murky water, whites appear to catch meals and thrive better than black crappies in the same environment.

Record White Crappies

The world record white crappie has stood at 5 pounds, 3 ounces since 1957. Fred Bright caught the slab in Mississippi.

Recent world line class records have included a 4-pound white crappie from Georgia and a 4-pound, 4-ouncer from Illinois. Recent world fly fishing records range up to 2 pounds, 8 ounces (from Virginia), and a 3-pound, 8-ounce world ice fishing record slab was taken in New York. The white/black hybrid crappie record is a 2-pound, 1-ounce hybrid caught in Lake Elizabeth in Wisconsin.

The typical state record white crappie weighs about 3 3/4 pounds, slightly larger than the black. Nearly a dozen and a half states have produced state record whites over 4 pounds, and at least four states—Mississippi, South Carolina, Tennessee and Georgia—have grown fish that officially weighed 5 pounds. Other top states that have grown giant white crappies include Oklahoma, Oregon, Texas, Alabama, California and Wisconsin. (Of the states which don't separate the species in their records, Louisiana leads, followed by North Carolina and Virginia.)

The oldest white crappie state record, at this writing, is South Carolina's 5-pound, 1-ounce fish, taken in 1949. One impressive recent record has been Georgia's 5-pound fish, caught in 1984. Other recent records include New York's 3-pound, 8 3/4-ounce white crappie, and Washington's 2-pound, 12-ounce white.

10

Finding And Catching Crappies

Crappies swim in a fascinating array of environments—from pockets in lily-pad patches to the bases of 50-foot-deep underwater rocky cliffs. It's no surprise anglers can't always find the fish—but that helps keep crappie fishing challenging and fun. Fortunately, for anglers, groups of crappies can be found at different cover and structure types at the same time in any given body of water.

To find crappies, an angler needs to be mobile. It's usually best to spend only several seconds at one particular submerged log or only 10 minutes within one area. If crappies don't appear, the successful fisherman moves. However, he may return to the same places later in the day, inspecting them during other light and water conditions.

Crappie location is linked to forage, cover (for feeding, protection or spawning), light, temperature, oxygen and other factors. During any season, crappies are generally more abundant in complex-structured areas such as drop-offs, pockets and points. Within this area, they often swim in or near cover or are on their way to cover, unless their main food source has lured them to open water. To help in the search, common tools include a contour map, a sonar unit, marker buoys, a thermometer and, to help you see underwater cover, polarized sunglasses.

Early Spring Locations

After the ice melts from Northern lakes or when the water

With crappies this size, it's small wonder that this team took the championship in a recent Crappiethon USA competition. Anglers can pull in fancy cash prizes catching crappies.

Finding And Catching Crappies

warms after the coldest period in the South, crappies at times swim into surprisingly shallow water, feeding on aquatic insect life and other forage. On warm, sunny days in reservoirs and natural lakes, including oxbow lakes, check cover along the north (warmer) shores, open water around future spawning areas, and at inlets and outlets. Small, first-to-warm lakes provide the top early action, and late afternoons are best, when the water's warmest. The water temperature may range from 30 to 50 degrees in the same lake, on the same day.

This relatively shallow water's woody objects—submerged trees, beaver houses and, where legal, manmade brush piles or stake beds—commonly attract the crappies. Thick cover isn't a necessity. A common situation is fish suspended in six- to eight-feet-deep water (shallower in dark water), maybe midway down near the cover.

Water clarity determines the distance you must keep from crappies. In murky tailwaters, you might catch fish from the bank right at your feet, but fishing a calm, murky lake from a boat usually means you should stay at least 10 feet away. In clear water, at least double the distance.

Thus, in clear water over shallow wood, whether you're shore or boat fishing, casting is the necessary method. A long sensitive rod, about 4- or 6-pound line, and a tiny jig—which snags less and which moves the slowest—is the right combination.

The jig (preferably $\frac{1}{16}$-ounce or less, if the wind allows) can be cast beyond the cover, and the retrieve and fishing depth are varied until you find what's best. For example, without reeling, let the jig drop with its own weight; then pull it very slowly so it "swims" over the limbs. The water's still cold so the retrieve must be at a snail's speed. Let it fall into holes, let it lie motionless, and scrape it against a log. As the jig is about to work out of the wood, let it slowly descend. If a fish hasn't hit it yet, bump the jig along the bottom at the tree's base like a little aquatic insect. Hits may be extremely delicate so watch the rod tip and the line very carefully.

If the water's on the murky side, you don't necessarily have to cast. With a long pole, you can dabble or flip baits or jigs to holes in the brush and trees or at stump sides and root areas. Six- or 8-pound line works fine if you use bendable hooks, though many anglers go heavier. In the thickest cover, simply pull the offering up to your pole's tip, then let it drop to where you think a crappie

Complete Angler's Library

holds. Bumping wood with the jig (or with the sinker on a minnow rig) helps attract the murky-water crappies which are more object-oriented than clear-water fish.

Bobber Presentation

Another tactic for clear or murky water is to cast with a bobber on the line. This way, larger jigs (or minnows) can work, too, and you have better control in wind. Floats limit the depth you fish, but they offer relatively snag-free fishing if they're set just above brush level. A well-known guide at Georgia's Weiss Lake (which has produced crappies over 5 pounds in the past) favors a jig/float combination during his favorite season, mid-February through mid-May.

Weiss Lake has lots of stumps and brush piles. It's basically a shallow lake—average depth about 7 feet—and normally you can't see deeper than 2 feet.

This guide will move slowly over crappie-filled flats looking for the woody cover, often three to six feet deep. He ties two tube jigs (containing some chartreuse) spaced apart below a tiny, thin float. He throws them out in an area where there's brush or stumps

Making Effective Weed Presentations

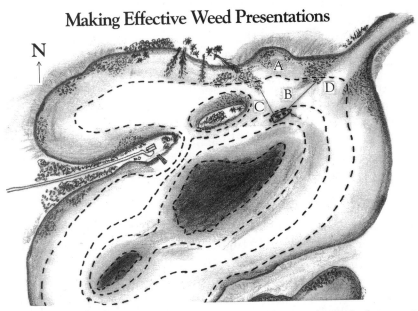

Identifying weed beds in a lake and then fishing them properly can pay big dividends in crappie catches. A boat is helpful because anglers can work the weed-bed edges more effectively.

and cranks it in steady, making a real slow presentation. Jigs with a weedguard are used to avoid hangups.

Catching Deep Early-Season Crappies

On colder days, warm-water discharges attract crappies. However, most lakes don't have this situation, and the angler usually needs to seek deeper water. Sonar helps find these fish and the appropriate structure and holes in bays or coves. On natural lakes, very slow drifting, trolling or vertical fishing can catch these deeper fish, frequently suspended near the structure. Offerings include jigs—light as possible—minnows or jig-and-minnow combinations. You can also long-cast over the school, retrieving through them.

To work the deep timber in reservoirs, it's best to fish vertically from a boat. A jig may work, but during these cold days, you may catch more with a bait-tipped jig. A sensitive rod is needed, and you need to watch the rod tip. Some anglers also make heavy catches using two minnows on a Kentucky Lake spreader rig. And few anglers jig hammered spoons.

Also, after ice-out or after the coldest period on a river or lake that doesn't freeze, check out small or medium feeder streams (at least 4 to 6 feet deep) which provide warmer water than the main body. Crappies, lured to the warmth and forage, hold in rock- or log-laden holes with little if any current.

The bait or lure needs to stay near the creek bottom; the favorite lure of a Minnesota creek fisherman is a $1/4$- or $1/8$-ounce jig or spinner. It's cast at an angle upstream of the fish, whose silver flashes are obvious in clear water.

Other creek methods include floating a jig or minnow below a clamp-on or slip bobber, and bottom-fishing with a heavy sinker and a lip-hooked minnow two or three feet below it.

Catching Rock Crappies

On larger rivers in spring, check eddies or slightly moving water below dams. During high-water winters, crappie may come down from the reservoir through the spillway, concentrating in the tailwaters. Also, warmer water coming from the dam can draw specklesides from downstream. The main cover often is riprap and boulders, which helps provide food and ambush points and relief from the current.

In Southern waters, a boat is often necessary in the winter because the fish are in deeper water. During warm spells, however, shore anglers can catch fish in surprisingly shallow water.

An excellent technique is to tie a jig (or two if legal) or minnow below a float. Cast upstream, let the rig float over the rocks, and then retrieve it slowly back. Or you can vertically jig or cast parallel with the riprapped shore without a float. A lightweight jig helps eliminate snags.

Rocks (and many other crappie sites) are ideal for European methods—use of long rods, 1- or 2-pound test line, a tiny, sensitive bobber and a tiny minnow or larvae-tipped jig. Casting or vertical fishing with such gear spooks fewer crappies, particularly in clear water.

Catching Pre-Spawn Crappies

As the days lengthen and water warms into the 50s and low 60s, lake crappies move toward spawning grounds. Pre-spawn fish

This summertime black crappie was holding near the rocks although the fish usually are found in deeper, cooler water. Wind had pushed plankton and minnows close to the rocky shore.

often hold near cover at drop-offs slightly deeper than the spawning sites. (The fish often spawn around the depth at which a water clarity disk disappears, although thick reeds can provide the cover for them to spawn shallower. To check clarity, you can use anything white and roughly plate-sized, such as an anchor painted white.) On warm days, look for cover in backwater areas, open water areas nearby, and inlets and outlets. If you can't see cover, clues to fish location include insects—commonly eaten at this time—and minnows near the surface.

Pre-spawn reservoir fish, on warmer days, move shallower and shallower along a cove's old creek channel. Also check inlets, outlets and cover-laden flats adjacent to these channels. Around March in southern impoundments, fish may be 20 feet down in cold weather, but in 50-degree water on sunny afternoons, you might catch fish around cover that's just a few feet deep. In super-clear reservoirs on warmer days, try fishing at or near cover around backwater coves, main-lake areas, islands and along the edges of creek channels.

On rivers, check tailwater eddies, and look for spawning cover in backwater sloughs and connected lakes. "Papermouths" will lurk nearby, their depth being dependent upon the weather. In any water on cold days, crappies commonly suspend away from the warm-day sites.

Catching Spawning Crappies

Once the surface temperature reaches the low 60s to low 70s, crappies generally move into relatively shallow water to spawn. On natural lakes, look for spawners on the north side first. Look for a bay, canal, an inlet or outlet, or even a plain bank with vege-tation, brush, logs, docks, trees and the like. Complex cover is a good starting point.

One method is to check the clarity using your boat anchor or whatever, and look for fish around that depth. But, at the same time, look toward shore for cover. If you encounter cover like bea-

Springtime crappies in natural lakes are often found in and around reed beds. The fish will hold close to the thicker clumps, and can be caught with jigs or minnows with or without a bobber.

Finding And Catching Crappies

ver huts for example, use the same tactics for wood described earlier. Often on natural lakes, however, crappies spawn around vegetation, commonly shallow-growing reeds. Use a long rod, a small jig and a float two or three feet above it. Work this slowly past thick reed masses. Also around the spawning period, fly fishing for crappies is at its best. Streamers or smaller flies can be effective, being dragged past the wood or weeds.

Polygamy occurs, so if you catch a heavy female at a reed clump one day, it's worth checking another day. Many anglers prefer to release spawners as over-fishing hurts crappie populations in some lakes.

While the shallows see most crappie movement, deeper adjacent water is a prime, overlooked spot. Yet-to-spawn crappies are staging there, and, in between egg-laying sessions, heavy females are there to rest and feed as long as food is available. Females in natural lakes habitually eat shiners, found throughout much of crappie territory. Shiners are a plankton feeder, a weed inhabitant and a fish which likes a pH around 8. Knowing the shiner's habits can help you find crappies.

On reservoirs, too, you can try for the deeper resting and feeding females. In Southern reservoirs, females often can be found near threadfin shad, a roaming forage fish which is sensitive to cold water, prefers a pH near 8.5, and tends to locate around plankton and bug larvae.

In murkier reservoirs and river backwaters, the shallower action takes place in water several inches to five feet deep. Clear-reservoir crappies do sometimes spawn more than 20 feet deep (deep channel turns can be great sites), but, as in natural lakes, if there's thick cover in shallower water, crappies frequently use it.

However, in reservoirs and rivers, water levels often fluctuate during spawning, complicating things. The spawning depth to look for is the one crappies used before the water level change as they'll hold to it until the nest is exposed.

Reservoir spawning commonly calls for shallow, woody cover tactics, including casting or dabbing at submerged brush, stumps, trees, bridge and dock posts, as well as grass and weeds.

One crappie angler and biologist dons waders and dangles a bait on a fly rod in cattails and woody cover. He feels he catches more crappies by doing so because the shoreline structure is so thick that it is difficult get a boat into where the crappie are.

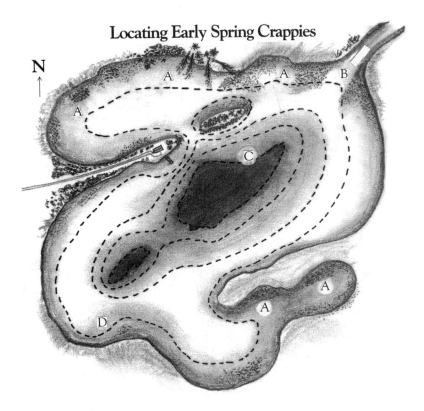

Locating Early Spring Crappies

The shallow areas marked A, B and D indicate some of the first places to look for early spring crappies. Shallow waters warm first, particularly on the north side of the lake (A), but don't forget edges of deep water where some large crappies may be holding (C).

Big-river spawners may gather near dam riprap, often in water 2 feet deep or shallower. Along large, old undammed rivers, spring means high water, and willows and brush near shore back in the chutes and oxbows lure big crappies. A top tactic is to *long-pole*, (vertical fish) a jig and minnow combo. Spawning Louisiana "sac-a-lait" are often taken anywhere from the surface to 4 feet deep in canals and bayous off the Mississippi River using a variety of cover woody methods.

Post-Spawn Crappies

Post-spawn crappies in all waters gradually move into the deeper summer haunts. Search the deep water nearest the spawning sites, near forage involving easy-to-catch prey, ranging from tiny fish to small crayfish to insects.

While recuperating from spawning, the fish aren't always easy to capture. On natural lakes, slow-troll or drift jigs or lipped-hooked minnows as you search with your sonar unit for suspended crappies at lake ends, bay centers or near down-lake points.

Post-spawners in clear mountain lakes may suspend 15 feet or deeper in cove middles, points and near main-lake woody bluffs. Crappies in dingy lakes, though, may remain more object-oriented in their post-spawn activities.

During post-spawn in rivers, the water usually lowers at the oxbows and sloughs. Using sonar and trolling the 10- to 15- foot-deep centers is best unless it's murky, and fish are swimming shallower in available woody cover.

Finding Summer Crappies

In summer, crappies feed actively and may be found near supplies of insects or small crayfish and, frequently, near good-sized baitfish. Surface-darting minnows can tip you off to crappies. And look for young bluegills and similar tiny fish, often found in a seven to eight pH. In the South, threadfin shad—and in turn crappies—will be following the drifting plankton.

When a thermocline forms, the crappies swim at or above it so they have sufficient oxygen. Oxygen readings, in fact, can provide excellent where-to clues: 4 parts per million or more is best.

Crappies in natural lakes frequently swim along weedlines, turns in drop-offs and at rock piles and humps.

In summer, rocks become moss-covered which attracts crappie forage. During low light, the fish may hover over the rocky hump or point, but during bright sun, they locate along the shady, rocky drop-off. Successful fishermen cast jigs, or if it's deep, vertically jig or minnow-fish, or troll. Good-sized minnows and lures work well at this time of year.

On weedy lakes, a top method is to slow-troll over the outside edge of cabbage or other aquatic weeds with a long line, concentrating on the shady, weedy drop-offs if the sun is bright. When you connect, you can switch to casting. Position the boat just outside the weedline. If there's a breeze, be just upwind of where the fish was, often at a pocket or point on the weed line. Cast over it, retrieving parallel with the weedline. Another method is to put a minnow or jig on a slip bobber rig and still or drift fish.

Crappies frequenting weedlines are usually roamers. If you lose contact, fish one direction down the weedline, then back the opposite way. However, if the skies are dimming, the specks may be shallows-bound. Cast toward shore from where you last caught fish with weedless lures like spinnerbaits.

Summer crappies also commonly surface in schools during dim conditions as they feed on insects or minnows. The tip-off is a rough patch on an otherwise smooth lake top. The only way to catch them is to long-line cast. The best gear is a long rod, 1- to 4-pound line, and any number of lures or baits—tiny jigs, spinners, spoons, flies and insect or minnow rigs suspended under a bobber all work well. It's not uncommon to catch and release a hundred or more fish on days crappies surface, using a slow retrieve.

Crappies In Summer Shade

Overhead cover allows summer crappies to swim shallow, even during sunshine. Bridges, swimming platforms, docks or thick surface weeds make the underlying water cooler and dimmer, and the cover attracts baitfish. Fish in clear reservoirs commonly find overhead cover under ledge rock at main-lake bluffs or along deep creek channel bends. The best overhead cover lies near drop-offs or deep, escape water at 10 or 25 feet or more, which is dependent on water clarity.

Any number of methods come into play, such as jigging while walking along the dock, vertically fishing minnows or jigs while your boat is tied to a bridge post or casting to pillars from shore. While it pays to fish the shadiest nooks, it may mean tight quarters, so jigs might need to be sling-shot under the dock or bridge. On the docks, fish vertically through the cracks in the boards which lie over the shadiest water. Or let the wind drift a minnow suspended under a bobber into the shade.

In some reservoirs, an "oxycline" forms in summer, and crappies swim above the lowest oxygen level. Overhead cover, such as a large marina dock, is especially attractive in this situation. In some murky reservoirs, crappies commonly swim in cover on flats or along the old river channel edges. One highly successful angler who fishes in a stained reservoir trolls at 15 feet deep or so, locating his largest slabs around brush piles and fencerows.

Irrigation can cause low summer water levels in some reservoirs. At one Nebraska reservoir in summer, crappie fishermen make good catches at the lower, main-lake riprap by the dam.

On many rivers in midsummer, crappies can be found on the surface during low light, but they're usually deeper. In medium-size streams, summer crappies hold on submerged timber in deep pools. You can find big-river backwater fish in deeper water around any timber or brush, or search the main channel, maybe 10 to 20 feet deep. At oxbows, check the centers during summer, and look for structure features just as in natural lakes.

Early Fall Crappies

When the water cools from the low 70s or 60s to the upper 50s, crappies scatter and can be found at various depths, including the easy-to-fish shallows. Fall food sources to watch for include shad, young bluegills, other small fish and crayfish.

On natural lakes, the first drop-offs and deep weedlines are prime places to find crappies in early fall especially at inside bends with cover. Rock piles and rocky islands can be hotspots, too, places where big crappies might find crayfish (which favor a pH near 7.5 in habitat offering a variety of animal and plant matter). During overcast or rainy conditions, five- to 10-foot water can offer top fishing and surfacing crappies might be spotted over these depths, but on bright days check about 15 feet deep. In these cases, trolling is a fast fish-finding method.

During early fall on murky reservoirs, cove-end stump fields under a few feet of water may begin to attract fish. But also check brush, rocks, logs and bridges near creek channel drops and on the main lake. In some clear-water reservoirs, crappies may not make much shallow early-fall movement so try the timber and rocks around deep (10 to 25 feet or more) main-lake or main-creek channel turns, points and islands.

Overhead cover such as docks and bridges can harbor numerous fall crappies on both natural lakes and impoundments. Best structures offer drop-offs and plentiful cover. Bridges over shallower water might attract fish in early autumn, but deep bridges are best later.

Draw-Down Crappies

On many reservoirs, fall signals a lowering water level, sometimes of several feet or more. (On big rivers, oxbows and sloughs may drop, too, and can be treated like draw-down in reservoirs.) Crappies, seven feet deep, may react by first heading for 12-foot

A bridge support in a natural lake was the scene of a battle with a fall crappie. The crappie was there to forage on young-of-the-year bluegills which were abundant at this spot.

Finding And Catching Crappies

water. At these times, brush piles and rocks at points and inside bends near the dam can be the hotspots. Jigs or minnow rigs fished deep while drifting or slow-trolling should score.

However, as the water cools into the 60s and upper 50s, forage fish such as threadfin shad work their way up shallower cove channels with crappies in pursuit. The shad can be picked up with electronics or seen on the surface. On other low-water reservoirs, forage species such as young perch may keep crappies deep.

A guide on the Potholes Reservoir in Washington state, for example, often finds during the fall a water clarity depth of two feet and water drawn down several feet, and crappies feeding on yellow perch about 2 inches long. The perch get out in the main lake when the water level drops low. They're right on the flat, sandy bottom, and the crappies are holding at 18 to 32 feet. Using a $1/16$-ounce silver mylar jig tipped with a maggot, this guide casts across the school, letting it fall in among the fish. He uses 4-pound, high-visibility line with a 3-foot clear leader (3- or 4-pound test) so the bigger black crappies can't see it.

If casting doesn't work, the guide drops the jig to the bottom, and raises it two feet. It's on a tight line, and as soon as there's a little "relief" or kind of a kink in the line, he advises to set the hook. If it really gets slow, he replaces the maggot with a crappie tongue. And, it's jigged real slowly in place with 2-pound test line.

Turnover Crappies

Late fall fishing begins with cold winds and rain turning a lake over, and it continues as the water temperature drops into the 40s and upper 30s.

Natural lakes turning over can make crappie fishing difficult. You might try fishing in cover near the outlets and inlets, or it may be best to fish a nearby river, especially around the riprap and other cover in the tailwaters below a dam—if the water is at least moderately deep.

Following turnover, on sunny days, the lake fish may move to somewhat shallow water. The warmer water on north sides of lakes might produce now, especially edges of live, green weeds. During colder periods, top clear-lake spots are bottlenecks between bay and main lake (especially at bridges) and warm-water inlets. Deep rock piles attract specklesides on weedy lakes after the weeds die. Trolling with a heavy jig works well.

When a reservoir gets colder, the main lake and warm-water discharges out-produce the coves. Bridges are good—if they're over deep water. On big-river backwater lakes, in early fall, one- to six-foot water may produce well, but later, think 10 or 20 feet.

Thick-Weed Crappies

On Southeastern weed-choked lakes, a productive location in fall (and winter) is thick aquatic weed beds a few to several feet deep. These beds contain minnows, freshwater shrimp and other common forage. Poke a stick in the weeds and stir out a hole. This commotion moves shrimp, and crappies are called in to feed. Simply lower a jig, shrimp or other offering. Moderately heavy line is necessary but that won't spook crappies because it blends in well with the weeds.

During winters cold-water period, specklesides are generally located at their deepest level of the year. The fish don't eat as much now, but there are some open-water winter patterns that can be successful. On natural lakes, hot spots include steep points, rock piles, humps, drop-offs at bay mouths and basin centers, often 20 or 30 feet deep. The fish, in tight schools, may be suspended in the open rather than in cover, and they respond to vertically presented minnows or bait-tipped jigs. In large rivers, many winter crappies migrate to backwater channels. During the most frigid weather, they migrate back to deep water, sometimes 30 feet down in the main river. During winter in murky Southern reservoirs, one expert locates crappies near trees in the eight-foot-deep creek basins or in small inundated lakes. (In warm winter weather, adjacent five- to six-foot deep channel banks hold fish, catchable with jigs or minnow/bobber rigs.) Deep water at cove mouths and bridges also hold fish, and warm-water discharges, if present, can be crappie magnets. In winter lakes like Toledo Bend, fairly clear for Southern reservoirs, crappies hold over the old river channel, which may be 80 feet deep. Suspended crappies, about 20 to 30 feet deep, can be nabbed with vertical presentations.

In the clearest mountain reservoirs, though most crappies swim higher, cold-water fish are sometimes caught on vertically fished minnows, jigs, or spoons more than 50 feet down along drop-offs—the most challenging of all crappies to find and catch.

=11=
Special Situations
For Crappies

The cold front that sweeps through your part of the country and the resulting bright blue sky and chilly north wind prompt crappies to "take the day off." This scenario happens with crappies more so than with many other species. Springtime crappies appear to be hardest hit, but fronts affect the fish during any season. Unfortunately, fronts sometimes appear every few days. A fisherman, however, can make fine catches during these periods if he knows how.

One angler recently studied 40 springtime crappie fishing trips in shallow to mid-depth water. The first and second days after a front are often thought to be the worst for fishing. However, in water below 55 degrees, the fronts didn't seem to affect shallow to mid-depth fish as much as when the water reached around 55 degrees or above. Below 55, more crappies were captured on the two post-front days than on the frontal day. This early in the year, sunlight is not direct enough to send the light-sensitive crappies into deeper water or thick cover. If the air isn't frigid, clear skies may warm the water in late afternoon enough to cause a positive crappie reaction. The angler's logbook showed a harvest of more than two times more crappie on clear days than cloudy.

When the water was about 55 degrees or warmer, cold fronts appeared to give shallow- to medium-depth anglers the worst blow. The logbooks showed best fishing at these depths came on cloudy or rainy days during passage of the front. However, catches fell off on the first and second days after the front. With the sun

During the warmer months, the shady side of a bridge or dock is one of the best places to find fish during a sunny day. If it's overcast, crappies may spread out in open water.

Special Situations For Crappies

higher now, bright skies seemed to be the culprit. If the weather remained stable, though, the third and fourth days proved to offer pretty fair fishing days.

Crappies in clear lakes are more affected by cold fronts so it can pay to travel to murky or moving waters. If you want some post-front fishing on a clear lake, try late-afternoon or night fishing or fish the darker water beneath a bridge or in deep water. Some crappies live deeper than others and are less affected by the front than shallower fish, so deep, woody cover along a reservoir's creek-channel drop-off or a natural-lake drop-off is an excellent choice. The depth may be 25 feet in clear water, 10 in murky. Fish that were located shallow or at mid-depths move down following the front.

Vertical Fishing Solves Cold Front Puzzle

Vertical fishing with a scented jig, small minnow or minnow-tipped jig is a top cold-front tactic. Offerings should be heavy enough, though, to put tension on the line so you pick up light hits

Fishing With Welding Rod Rigs

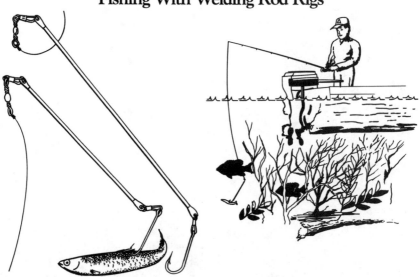

Anglers working heavy, brushy cover in search of crappies will use a stiff, heavy leader such as this welding rod rig. The ends of the rod are flattened and a hole drilled in each end for attaching line and hook. It is easier to pull loose of snags and keep the fish free of tangles.

Working Clear and Murky Waters

CLEAR

MURKY

When working cover in clear water (top), you must stay far enough away so your boat doesn't spook the fish. In murkier water, you can work in close, often jigging vertically into cover.

better. Light line—6-pound test or lighter if you can get by with it—is best. It pays to fish different depths—very slowly—and to stay close to cover, especially at shallower depths. Cold-front fish can also be caught by slow-trolling or drifting. If legal, use at least a couple small jigs or a Kentucky Lake (tandem hook) minnow rig.

Catching Crappies In The Wind

Any month, and especially in spring, when most crappie anglers hit their favorite waters, there are usually breezes and wind gusts to deal with. Wind can play havoc when casting, and bites can be almost impossible to detect. Fortunately, there are several ways to cope and still make heavy catches. You can also take advantage of the wind by using the drifting method, and the wind might even tell you where and when to fish.

If whitecaps rise so high that fishing from a boat is dangerous, shore fishing can still be feasible. First, find an area not being barraged; you'll find it easier to detect bites here. A small lake, pond or a steep-sided river channel may offer the only such site. Ideal spots are where crappies swim near shore; look for visible cover, a weedy drop-off that swings close to shore or whatever seems appropriate for the time of year that you're fishing.

You can take advantage of a back wind by casting a jig or other offering high in the air, thus achieving great distances and enabling you to cover more water. You can also cast a bobber rig and let it neatly float through the crappie schools. With a side wind, you can short-cast first, let the bobber make its drift and then cast out at increasing distances to cover every inch. Bite detection is more difficult in the wind, so it helps to use tricks that make crappies hold onto your offering longer. Consider using bait instead of artificials, or when using artificials, choose soft lures and squirt on panfish attractant. Also, use extra thin, sharp hooks to allow many of the fish to hook themselves.

Drifting Takes Advantage Of Wind

Boat-fishing in the wind with any safe-size boat can also produce. If you can safely anchor, you can cast as mentioned. But winds also allow you to employ one of the deadliest crappie fishing methods—drifting.

Drifting is a quiet method; it spooks fewer fish than when you make the same pass with a small outboard back-trolled or even a trolling motor. A boat in the waves is also less noticeable to fish than a boat in calm water. The boat may appear as a large floating tree, and your lures resemble food drifting by at natural speed.

When drifting, locate crappie cover or structure—a riprapped shore or a weedy drop-off which lies parallel with the wind so you spend more time in the fish zone. A trolling motor can help maintain the proper line of travel if necessary or, if you're using a small boat, a paddle is a quiet substitute. Hold the paddle in the water so it's vertical and still; no paddling is necessary. Simply turn the paddle to rudder the boat in the desired direction. You can handle a fishing rod in your other hand. As crappies always require a slow lure/bait presentation, you can slow your boat's drift by putting your paddle crossways against the water, or by tossing out a sea anchor such as one or more five-gallon pails tied to a rope attached securely to your boat.

Often in wind in the warm months, crappies swim fairly shallow and a long-line-fished minnow or light jig produce the best. A bobber usually shows you strikes better than a wind-whipped rod tip. Deep crappies can be fished directly below the boat with heavier jigs or extra weight and a slip bobber when baitfishing. If legal,

Crappies will normally choose a spawning site on the bottom at a depth around or slightly below where a white disk or an anchor painted white disappears when lowered into the water.

fishing with several rods helps you to find the best spots more quickly by fishing different depths.

Wind And Crappie Location

Wind can also show you where to locate crappies. In spring, a warm south wind warms up the north shore, and warm temperatures are what cold-water crappies love. But in later months, also consider going to any wind-hit area. The wind pushes plankton which small fish—crappie food—feed on. If the water is 70 degrees, there'll be abundant plankton near the surface, and if there's a westerly wind for a couple days, an east-shore area could hold many crappies. Crappies often stay at one spot as long as there's food around. If the wind is excessive, many minnows or other forage may move deeper rather than be drifted, but enough food is still bound to be pushed into the area.

Wind not only pushes food toward shore; it also creates crappie cover—a debris pile. You might try casting along the pile edges in hopes your offerings attracts edge-holding crappies. Another option is to let the wind push the boat into the cover. The debris eventually anchors the boat. Take your rod and reel or, often better, a 10- to 15-foot pole and dabble lures and baits through any holes. Poke holes if none exist. Some anglers cast an $1/8$-ounce jig violently enough into the debris so it penetrates.

Winds can also tell you when to fish. As mentioned, when the water's cool, in the 50s or lower, a south wind tells you to hit the water. At higher temperatures, according to angler tests conducted during 100 crappie outings, south winds can mean pretty good fishing, but if they blow continuously for a few days or more, fishing appears to slow.

North winds, when the water reads in the 50s or 60s, generally indicate tougher fishing and you'll be required to use cold-front tactics. After the water warms past the upper 60s, though, these winds have less of an effect and some days north winds are accompanied by quite easy fishing.

Westerly and easterly winds can bring varying results, often good in 50- and 60-degree water. Calm-water fishing, according to the tests, proved best in 50s water during warm fronts.

You can adjust predictions with water level fluctuations, lunar activity tables and so on, but the wind can often be the best tip-off to good fishing times.

Catching Crappies At Night

An owl, invisible in the darkness, hoots out as you slowly boat to a bridge. At a bridge post, you light a lantern and, before long, bugs and baitfish fight for space in its beam. A minnow submerged on a hook immediately brings a tap, and you haul in your prize—a night-feeding slab crappie.

Crappies commonly feed after the sun goes down, yet many lakes across the country see little or no night-fishing pressure. Though the practice isn't allowed on a few waters, night-time delivers heavy catches at times, no matter the season.

Night-owl crappies might nab minnows and jigs even when you don't use an artificial light; the fish see fairly well after their eyes adjust to the darkness. Boating on lakes lit solely by the

It can be hot fishing on many crappie lakes, especially clear ones, after the sun goes down. Crappies prefer the cover of darkness and can be caught at night during any season.

moon, you can sometimes spot surfacing crappies. Casting to the fish with slow-moving jigs or minnow/bobber rigs provides unusual sport. However, fishermen can catch more fish by employing brighter lights.

Mercury or other lights on shore and at docks and bridges often attract microorganisms and, in turn, minnows or shad which crappie want. Often more effective, though, is a lantern or crappie light, placed on or beneath the lake surface. When lantern fishing, if insects are a problem, you can hang the light out away from the boat. Special brackets are available for this. An aluminum foil shield keeps the light from glaring into your eyes.

A crappie light—in a sealed-beam light floating, styrofoam holder—is preferred by many night anglers. One or two lights are connected to a 12-volt battery, and they may shoot out around

25,000 candlepower. Halogen fishing lights are brighter, putting out over 200,000 candlepower. Because these lights can be completely submerged, they may pull in fewer bugs than do the usual above-water lights.

Other night-time gear includes insect repellent, a flashlight, sensitive graphite rods or poles (some come with high-visibility tips), and, if you prefer bobber fishing, high-visibility floats (some light up) and 6-pound-test monofilament.

Crappie minnows are the most common night baits. Minnows or small shad caught from the lake you're fishing on often can't be beat. In summer, when they're hatching, adult mayflies, one or two on a crappie hook, are often the best bait. Jigs can work, too, with many night anglers favoring black or white jigs because crappies may not see color well at night. The black offers the most contrast against the fishing light or the sky. Against the dark water, white jigs with or without phosphorescence can work well. You may buy jigs already painted with the glowing substance or you can stick on luminescent tape.

Finally, before heading out, it's important to make sure the running lights, wiring and electrical equipment are in reliable, working condition. A slow boat ride using a depthfinder turned on helps you find your crappie hole safely.

Locating Crappies At Night

Crappies might be located at night near their daytime haunts, but they're often a bit shallower. In spring, when crappies are shallowest, nightfishing is least popular because the fish can be easy pickings in daytime. In summer on many lakes, though, nightfishing becomes more popular and is an excellent way to beat the heat. Clear water crappies, especially, may be difficult to catch on a summer day, but they're more accessible to anglers at night. In summer, it pays to keep in mind the thermocline level. If it's 25 feet, they may be near this level. But, some fish are still bound to be shallower, especially at night. Fall and winter (including ice-covered lakes) can be great times to nightfish with minnows or jigs. Think shallower in fall and deeper in late fall and winter.

To locate fish, look for fishermen, or search around woody cover, docks or bridges. You can call in crappies with lights, but it's best to check out an area first with sonar. Others set out brush piles at good nighttime spots and head straight for them. Some hang a sack of chum such as bread to attract extra minnows around the sunken timber or concrete bridge posts.

Minnows can be fished vertically at night. Some anglers prefer to use a bobber, but currents or waves often float the bobber away from the crappie-holding spots. Jigs can be cast into the dark and very slowly retrieved into the light. Some crappies may hit at the illuminated area's edges (especially if the light is bright), and others right below the lights. One level is usually better than others, but that depth can change during the night. Keeping the sonar unit on alerts you to a change quickly.

Fishing is usually tops on dark nights, but even then, the action isn't at a constant pace. You may sit there an hour or two and not get a hit. But then at 10 o'clock, one in the morning or who knows when, you might run into all the night-owl crappies you can handle.

Catching Suspended Crappies

Many anglers associate crappies with brush piles or weeds; however, crappies often suspend off the bottom a short distance from cover or way out in open water.

Fishermen's noise or large predator fish may have caused this suspending, and, sometimes, crappies simply are resting in the open water, and not moving much (perhaps, after finishing feeding). In these cases, the fish may be difficult to catch.

But crappies also hit the mid-depth open water when they're hungry and on their way to food sources. They move through the open water, hitting a brush pile here and rocky island there. Often, the forage itself—minnows, shad, zooplankton—is suspended, and the crappies are feeding. These are favorable fishing conditions usually resulting in large stringers.

Crappies may suspend during any month. In spring, crappies often hover over deeper water near spawning areas. After the spawn, especially during daylight, many crappies suspend in cove or bay centers. In summer and fall, crappies are famous for suspending in shady drop-offs, outside Northern-lake weedlines, at the centers of Southern oxbows, and other dark spots, often below the heaviest plankton and minnow level. (Plankton requires a certain amount of light so this baitfish forage—and thus baitfish, too—can live deeper in clear water than in dark water. Some plankton moves up and down with the changing light levels during the day, and crappies are there to intercept them or the bait-fish.) Winter crappies commonly hover over very deep water.

Using sonar is the easiest method to find fish; suspended crappies show up well. You don't always need to look for the crappies, though. If you see balls of baitfish on the screen, that's reason enough to try for suspended fish in the area.

A graph recorder can show you crappies better than other sonar, but other units can work well, too, as long as the unit is turned to the proper sensitivity to pick up the details. Horizontal marks inside a ball of baitfish may well be crappies, or the fish may appear as a thick mass of larger marks (hooks) below or to the side of the baitfish. There may be straggler crappies many yards away, but there's usually a main crappie school. The school's depth from top to bottom may be wider on clear lakes than murky lakes and may be in vertical form. White crappies in a school are known to be more spread out (horizontally) than black crappies. However, if there's a food concentration or if an angler has put the fish into a feeding frenzy, whites may group tightly, too.

With sonar, note the depth and the school's thickness to determine top fishing depth. Also, it pays to watch how the fish are relating to a nearby weed-line or channel edge; it might be a pattern to look for later. Place marker buoys over the structure and at fish schools to keep on top of them.

In open expanses without structure—common on shallow lakes—marker buoys should still be dropped when fish are located. Crappies not near structure or cover are generally roamers so drop another buoy if you start catching fish off to one side. That might give you an indication of the school's direction.

Finding Suspended Fish Without Sonar
A Washington state guide uses a graph to find crappies, but for anglers without sonar, he suggests casting a small sinking minnow-imitating crankbait, counting one-thousand-one, one-thousand-two, and so on, until a fish hits.

Here's how to do it. If you're in about 22 feet, throw it about 10 feet, about half way, and the crappies will come up for it and you can locate them that way. If you do hook one, he adds, come back through the same area. If you hook another one, throw your marker buoy.

Suspended crappies can be caught by vertical, slip-bobber and

164   Complete Angler's Library

When you get into a bunch of crappies, the action can be fast and furious. These fish were hitting a $^1/_{16}$-ounce jig, cast and slowly retrieved over rocks in water six feet deep.

Special Situations For Crappies

cast-and-retrieve presentations as detailed earlier. But, trolling comes more into play when the fish suspend; you're often away from snags so you can troll easily. Trolling, though, is still an option when fish suspend near or around cover such as stumps which don't produce quite as many snags as brush and trees.

Trolling works well even if you're allowed to fish only one rod. In some states, though, you may fish with an unlimited number, in which case anglers commonly troll with 10 or 15 poles, called spider-rigging. The extra baits in the water make this an excellent fish-finding method in itself.

Some prefer to hand-hold rods while trolling. Multi-pole trollers employ rod holders, usually placing longer poles off the boat's sides. If these poles are 14 feet long, you can cover a band of water about 30 feet wide or more in one pass. Shorter poles and rods can be used to cover the inside water.

Six-pound line is the choice of many crappie trollers, but since snags aren't a big problem, 2- or 4-pound line may result in more fish. Some prefer plain-line trolling, but small floats on the line offer more-visible strikes.

Baits or lures for trolling include lip-hooked minnows or artificials like jigs. In murkier waters, though, larger artificials like crankbaits and spoon-type lures are more visible and may produce well. If more than one lure is used, it's best to set them out at different depths to test more water.

To Catch Crappies

A quiet electric trolling motor on a boat of about 14 feet in length can be ideal for crappie trolling. It's less noisy than back-trolling with a small outboard. Whatever is used, fishing slowly is important, though you might go a little faster in summer.

One approach is to zig-zag just outside the drop-off, weedline, around an island or other areas where crappies suspend. Shorelines sometimes have two or more "breaks"—maybe a weedline and then one or two drop-offs, and it can pay to troll them all. One thing to keep in mind is that the lures way out behind the boat aren't necessarily running over the same water depth as the sonar unit's transducer. If the transducer is following a submerged point's contour, the lures will miss that important pocket water near the point, where the fish may well be suspended. An angler needs to travel up over the point a ways to make sure the lures hit that pocket in order to increase his chances of catching fish.

If you see crappies on the sonar and they're rather shallow, the best tactic is to speed up so the offerings get shallower. Then, slow down to allow the lures to drop into the school.

For fish suspended deeper, an alternative to long-line trolling is to slow-troll baits or lures directly below the boat. This is a hot method for a crappie guide on Alabama/Georgia's Weiss Lake. In the fall, he fishes towards the dam where there are ledges which are relatively deep for that lake. The top of the ledge may be nine or 10 feet deep and, where it drops into the river channel, 30 feet deep. But, he doesn't fish any deeper than about 12 feet, until the water temperature goes down below 50 degrees.

He makes a L-shaped bend in an aluminum pipe so that it will stick out from the side of the boat about six feet and point down. A transducer is attached to the end of the pipe, pointing straight down. Then, he lines up cane poles right behind the transducer all the way down one side of the boat. He trolls into the wind to control the boat and watches the sonar. When he finds a stump, he puts out a marker. If the top of that stump is nine feet deep, he can just ease his rods up to about eight feet deep or so, and the minnows are right in the strike zone.

Downrigging For Crappies

Downrigging is a little-used method for crappies, but it can be effective on suspended fish. Downriggers allow precise depth control which is not always possible with long-line trolling. You can also make sharp turns, turning more quickly, and still be effective.

A downrigger (a simple, low-priced one works well) consists of a cable reel, cable arm and cable. At the cable's end is a cannonball weight of 6 pounds or better. Near the ball is a line-release snap. When a crappie hits, the snap releases the fishing line so you can play the fish. Common trolling baits or lures might be used; however, even lures not usually thought of as deep-water offerings, such as spinners, can produce exceptionally well. You don't want the lure close to the ball; about 30 feet behind is better. Also, while you can use downriggers in five feet of water, they're at their best for catching crappies in deeper water.

Yellow Perch

12

All About
Yellow Perch

According to a famous football coach, "Know your opponent, and the game's half won before you start." He had a point there, and the same holds true for perch. Knowing something about how this doughty little warrior lives and grows can give insight into how to fish for and catch him. For openers, scientific types have labeled the yellow perch, Perca flavescens. Perca, for what it's worth, means "dusky," and flavescens translates from Latin as "becoming gold colored." They are closely related to walleyes and saugers—all members of the perch family. Yellow perch are also known as river perch, ringed perch, raccoon perch, lake perch, American perch, striped perch and jack perch.

Perch are greenish-brown or simply dark green along their back, shading to yellow green or yellow along the sides, and white on the belly. Their belly fins are often yellow to reddish, and they have two sets of dorsal fins. The forward pair have spines sharp enough to break skin if a you're not careful. Add sharp areas on their opercle flaps (gill covers) that can also roughen or even cut human skin, and you've a good description of the perch.

They're a distinctive fish, and are unlikely to be mixed up with other species, especially when you add those bold, blackish vertical bands along their sides.

Perch were originally found over a huge slice of the East, the Midwest and Northern states, and well into Canada's provinces. Now, they're spread far wider. Stocking efforts have expanded

When knowledgeable pier fishermen go for perch, their main weapon in their fishing tackle arsenals are small, white jigs with white tails. These are sometimes called doll flies.

All About Yellow Perch

their range as far south as New Mexico and Texas, west to Washington, Oregon and a small segment of California, and east to Maine and South Carolina. Today, there are few states that don't have perch in at least a lake or two, and these versatile little fish are still spreading.

World Record Catch In 1865

In the marine world, perch are small fish, with the average caught in most states running 7-to-10 inches. But, in the world of panfish, they do grow fairly large. The world record perch, a 4-pound, 3-ounce lunker, came from the Delaware River in New Jersey. However, it was caught back in 1865. These days, you're not likely to catch a 4-pound-plus perch, but, there are plenty of spots where a 2-pounder or even a 3-pounder can turn up.

Typically, it takes a magical combination of plentiful food and large water area to produce big perch. The bounty of food causes fast growth, and larger lakes provide a fish with a reasonable chance to grow without being caught. A dandy could be taken from a two-acre lake if that body of water were rarely fished. But, that's unlikely in most states.

Lots of big lakes produce lunker perch. Eastern Lake Erie, particularly off Ashtabula and Conneaut, Ohio, is becoming known for having lots of big perch, and Lake Ontario also has its full share. The Charity Islands in Michigan's Saginaw Bay annually produce large fish, as does Mille Lacs Lake in central Minnesota. Then, there's Devil's Lake in North Dakota, and plenty more. Information on your state's lakes that hold big perch is easy to come by. Just ask the people at your state's fisheries department. They'll have plenty of suggestions.

Fillets Excellent Eating

Some people wonder why perch are such a hard-sought fish by so many anglers of both sexes, all ages and all walks of life. The answer is simple: It's a fun fish that can be caught by anyone with a minimum of gear and a minimum of effort. Wherever perch swim, you'll find people trying to catch a bucket of these excellent eating fish. You'll find a wide assortment of poles, rods and reels, usually a bucket of minnows, perhaps a folding chair and radio, some sandwiches and cold drinks. That's because perch fishing generally is an easy-going business.

Yellow Perch

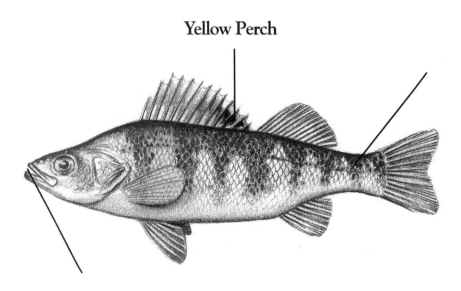

Yellow perch have yellow sides and six to nine black or olive vertical bars on the each side. They lack canine teeth. Adults have a dusky markings between the last four spines of the dorsal fin.

With gear arranged on a handy pier and a couple of minnows swimming in the business zone below, it's time to relax and talk to fellow anglers, or to share insights with a young son or daughter or a growing family. Until that rod tip suddenly begins to bounce, signaling a customer on the other end. Then, it's time to haul up a modest little fighter or two, rebait, and go back to whatever the angler was doing before. Until the next perch bites. Still, you'll quickly recognize the serious perch fisherman who wants to fill a stringer every time out.

Perch have a lot going for them besides being generally easy to catch. One, they're prolific so many lakes, upground reservoirs and slow-moving streams have thousands or perhaps millions of these hungry panfish. Two, they're usually schooling fish, and easier to catch in large numbers. Occasionally you will find just one, and that's when the fish are suspended.

And three, they're excellent eating. The perch fits the word "panfish" as well as, and perhaps better than any other species. Their flesh is white and succulent, and diners from San Francisco to Miami and New York have sunk eager teeth into broiled fillets, with side dishes, or butterflied fillet sandwiches.

Gourmet Prices For Perch

In fact, since perch fillets routinely sell for $5 to $6 or even more per pound in fish shops and supermarkets, they're one species you can actually make a profit on. Consider time, gas money and bait; then, compare the poundage of fillets in the freezer. That fishing trip could have produced a profit of several dollars an hour. But, perch should never be fished for profit, rather for relaxation, good companionship, family fun and delectable fillets. They're *Everyman's* fish.

Perch haven't always enjoyed such a good reputation as a great eating fish. Read some of the old books, and it quickly becomes obvious that the prime culinary fish of the early 1800s was muskellunge, with perch ranking alongside rough fish such as carp and sheepshead. In fact, one early writer described perch flesh as soft and insipid, with a coarse texture. Another noted that they were free for the taking from fish dealers who picked them up in nets along with more desirable species. Yet a third told of selling three tons of perch as manure to a farmer for a dollar a ton.

It is doubtful that perch were less tasty then, or that muskies of that day were better than they are now. It simply shows that tastes change. The perch's reputation as a fine table fish is unquestioned in the 1990s.

Adaptable Perch

Yellow perch are found in a wide variety of habitats. They're very widespread in the Great Lakes, excluding Lake Superior, big waters that range from cold to moderately warm. They like upground reservoirs, those high-rising city water supplies so common through the Midwest, and they're found in small, warm-water, weedy lakes, or equally in cold northern lakes with sand and marl bottoms. They're common in some slow-moving rivers, too, especially deep pools, but the ideal habitat for perch is a cool water lake with moderate amounts of vegetation, reasonable fertility and a bottom that's a fair mixture of sand, mud, gravel and boulder patches. Bottoms with an occasional weed bed give perch all they need in terms of food and cover.

Perch begin their life cycle somewhere between mid-March and early May, depending on when ice goes out on their home lake and when water temperatures reach 45 to 52 degrees. They prefer quiet bays, backwaters or sloughs for spawning, and nor-

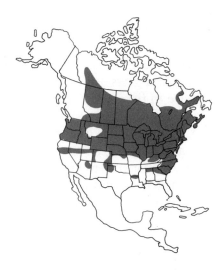

Yellow perch are found in most of the Northern states and a few areas in the South as well as throughout much of Canada.

mally choose depths of two to four feet. If the spot has submerged vegetation or brush to receive the eggs, it is an ideal spawning place for perch.

Typically, perch elect to spawn at night, and usually the business is conducted by a single, large-bellied female, and a long line of males, up to 15 or 20 in some cases. The female glides along, and the males follow, occasionally bumping the female until she drops her strands of eggs which are immediately fertilized by the eager males who are close by.

The strands carry anywhere from 1,000 up to 200,000 eggs, depending on the size of the female. Adult perch have no further interest in their eggs or young, depending on vast numbers of eggs to provide the required survivors.

The young perch, however, face a hazardous life. Hatching eight to 10 days after spawning in normal water temperatures, they're at first clumsy and uncoordinated, easy prey for juvenile walleye, sunfish or even other perch, and predatory insects. But the remainder feed avidly on zooplankton creatures, teeming freshwater crustaceans, from copepods to cladocerans and ostracods, and the perch grow rapidly.

Perch often reach 3 inches in length in a single year. Then, adding aquatic insects to their diet, young perch grow more

All About Yellow Perch

slowly, routinely reaching 5 inches at the end of their second year, and 7 or 8 inches during the third. Fish doesn't become a major food item for perch until well into the second year.

Perch Feed Heavily On Insects

Most anglers use minnows and, occasionally, worms but nothing else in fishing for perch. But, evaluation of stomach contents has shown that perch feed more heavily on insects than anything else, at least where insects are abundant. They like aquatic fly larvae, and mayflies at any time. Caddis flies in the larval stage are eaten in quantity, as are a number of other insects from dragonfly nymphs to chironomids.

Fish, mostly minnows, rank second on the perch's hit list, followed by odds and ends like crayfish, fish eggs, snails and plant matter. It's a key to the perch's success, this willingness to feed on whatever food is available. If one menu item is lacking, they'll turn the page to another. And continue growing.

Perch Are Short On Brains

A good deal of perch behavior, movements and feeding tactics stems from their evolution as a schooling-type prey fish, rather than a solitary or small group predator. Schooling species have a tendency toward low I.Q., which makes them far easier to catch than serious predators. An Ohio State University study demonstrates that fact perfectly. In the study, fish from large- and smallmouth bass to pike, perch and white bass were placed in large tanks. Each tank was divided with a partition in which a modest sized hole had been cut. Then, the fish were given time to become accustomed to the tank, the partition and the hole. After a few days, various-shaped bits of wood were lowered into the tank. Only one shape was "dangerous." When it was lowered, the fish received an electrical shock about 15 seconds later. Unless, that is, they hurriedly swam through the hole to the tank's other side where they were safe.

The smallmouth bass learned astonishingly fast. After a very few trials and shocks, the whole cluster of bass would race to the other side as soon as the dangerous shape hit the water. The largemouths learned a little slower. The half dozen or so yellow perch never learned at all. They were smart enough to know that when the dangerous shape came, they were in trouble, but they would freeze rigid, flaring gillflaps and raising dorsal fins in self defense. They never learned to escape and avoid the shock.

Why are schooling fish less intelligent than others? Many scientists believe that these types depend heavily on each other for protection. A tight school will often be circled but not attacked by a finned predator who perceives it to be one large creature, rather than many small ones. Also, in a school, there are hundreds of eyes to seek out danger, hundreds of lateral lines to pick up predator vibrations, hundreds of potential targets that diminish the chance of any individual being taken. You don't need to be smart to survive as part of a large school. Solitary predators, on the other hand, must live by their wits or die.

Schooling often enhances feeding success, and helps the perch survive, too. A loose school of perch moving slowly across a rocky bottom maintains a lightly scattered position where terrain permits. Each individual fish may be anywhere from 6 inches to several feet from his nearest neighbor. Individuals dart here and there in the murky water, their large eyes sensitive enough even at fair depths to see crawling insects moving over the rocks, minnows foraging for plankton or a crayfish that is flushed from beneath a small stone.

As long as food is scattered, they'll feed comfortably. The school will remain on this gravel flat feeding on mayfly larvae until they're gone, then move slowly along to nose around a cluster of boulders. When a concentration of food is found, a beginning hatch of midge, perhaps, or a fair-sized school of minnows, the fish close in tighter and feed avidly, surrounding and confusing their prey, which find perch waiting to eat them no matter in which direction they flee.

Perch have other behavioral quirks that anglers should know and understand, if they wish to increase their catch. For example, unlike some species including trout and salmon, the perch handles minimal oxygen nicely, and even survives winter kill conditions that wipe out bass, bluegill and walleye. Perch do most of their feeding on or very near bottom, though they'll rise somewhat if food is abundant above them. If they have to go into water that's nearly devoid of oxygen, they'll do so.

That eliminates a favorite tactic of anglers in general which is finding the thermocline and either fishing just above it, after oxygen levels sink below in late summer, or seeking water shallow

Pier fishing can be very productive if pier anglers remember basic tactics and study perch behavior. Fan casting and jigging along the pier and tight in around uprights pay dividends.

enough to be above the thermocline. Perch will feed mostly on the bottom, no matter where the thermocline is. They're tough fish to kill in terms of temperature, too. They can handle water that's 90 degrees or more, as well as survive salinity levels that can reach 10 parts per million.

Perch School By Size

But it's their schooling behavior that's most important to a hungry angler. Studies have shown that schools, which generally run from 40 up to 250 fish, tend to stick together in accordance to age and size. So fish tend to be mostly of one general length. Small perch favor shallow water with vegetation which provides good protection from predators, so schools of youngsters are likely to be found in these places. Larger perch, which are safer from walleye and pike, tend to prefer open water, sometimes territory well off-shore, so good-sized keepers are most often found there. Since individuals often leave a school and move elsewhere, it's not unusual to catch an occasional straggler even in a bad spot, but anglers must find fair-sized schools to ensure a nice catch.

Movements during the day are important, too. In Wisconsin's Lake Mendota, for example, scientists studying perch movements found that during summer daylight hours, the fish swim in large schools at depths between about 25 and 35 feet. As sundown approaches, they move shoreward until they touch bottom. Then, they cruise at depths of around 20 feet until the sun sinks. At this point, they drop to the sand and lay motionless until daylight, at which time they form into schools again, moving back into deeper water. Good information to keep in mind the next time you're seeking perch.

13

Finding And Catching Perch

W hen NAFC members fish lakes of any type, it's important to remember that perch schools do not remain stationary. You'll catch them here one week, and in another spot half a mile away the next. Each season of the year also has its own subtleties when it comes to perch location. Knowing where to expect to find perch in a given season is vital to making a good catch.

In early spring, for example, when perch are moving shallow for spawning, they can be found along shallow breaks close to shore. Pier fishermen do extremely well not long after ice-out on these pre-spawn fish, and boat anglers routinely catch them in six, or even four feet of water. It's a very good time to take lunkers since the biggest fish, which spend most of their time in deep water, are in areas where they are relatively easy to find.

Perch remain in shallow water for several weeks after the spawning ritual, then gradually migrate toward greater depths. In shallow lakes, they might summer in 15 to 20 feet of water, while in deeper ones they'll gather around submerged islands, rocky shoals, points and other cover in water 20 to 30 feet deep, even more. Then, in the fall they move shallow again, coming into water of eight to 15 feet in lakes of no great depth, slightly deeper in lakes of more depth. In winter, many lakes will hold fish at depths of 20 to 30 feet.

It points out again the fact that a fishermen must come to know his lake, and be willing to move until he finds perch, search-

A jumbo perch always brings a smile to an angler's face, especially when the angler has success-fully tracked the perch in open water and can look forward to landing more that size, as well.

Finding And Catching Perch

ing both shallow and deep water as necessity dictates. But, the general rule is shallow in early spring, deep in summer, fairly shallow in fall, slightly deeper in winter.

Yellow perch move during the day, as well as during a season, and that movement is basically from deep to shallower water where there's good bottom structure and good feeding grounds, then back again. And they do much of their food-seeking early and late in the day. This is why action can be so hot over the first and last hours of daylight, and frequently slack in the middle of each day. Baiting up at 11 a.m. for a couple of hours fishing isn't the answer on most trips.

Remember, too, that while perch will hug bottom closely during any season, studies have shown that on some occasions they will suspend, for whatever reason. Suspended fish are likely to be

Rigs For Finding Perch

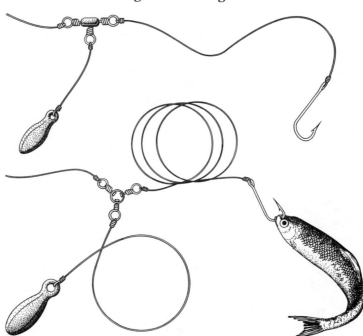

These two swivel rigs are good for going after bottom-holding perch. The upper illustration shows an in-line swivel in which the swivel allows the weight to bounce freely without twisting the line. Below is three-way swivel rig, another way of presenting bait on the bottom.

A tandem rig with two hooks above a sinker is a powerful combination in some waters, particularly when going after perch like this pair taken from Saginaw Bay on Lake Huron.

loafing, rather than feeding, but they'll still often hit a bait. In short, hit the bottom first, but if that fish locator shows schools of fish swimming well above, try them. Many a fisherman has limited out because he discovered the fish were up, rather than down, and made the knowledge pay off.

Other Tips And Tactics For Perch

Movements of individual perch often excite an entire school, and an angler can take advantage of this fact. When a shiner minnow is lowered into a lazily feeding school, then taken by a hungry fish, that perch's struggles and gyrations as it disappears upward, seem to be taken as a sign of good feeding by his fellows. So, other minnows that spiral down are taken more quickly, and the school gathers tightly to feed on the manna from above. Until the school

Finding And Catching Perch

finally spooks, or moves off. It makes for easy fishing, and fast filling of nets or coolers.

You can actually speed the process by dropping some dead shiners now and then. In any minnow bucket, there are sure to be a few minnows either dead or nearly so floating on the top. Dropping these by the handful into the feeding zone below, with attendant glittering scales is sure to stimulate renewed feeding interest. Be sure to squeeze the dead minnow to empty its air bladder, allowing it to sink. Some anglers go even further and, where it's legal, lower frozen blocks of dead shiners in a mesh net to keep bits of bait and scales flowing. An occasional jerk on the line will scatter even more tidbits and draw in perch from yards away.

Is there a cast-in-granite technique for finding perch throughout the seasons? Not really. In early spring when they're spawning, you can be reasonably sure of finding them in shallow water, those aforementioned bays and backwaters where there's brush and weeds to drape their long strings of gelatinous eggs. Or at least along shores that are fairly well protected from wind and have the necessary cover. Otherwise, their presence depends on adequate food supply.

Perch Love Mud Bottoms

According to a top Ohio fisheries biologist, perch are strictly opportunists. In Lake Erie, for example, the biologist has found that they forage heavily throughout most of the year on soft mud bottoms. Soft mud bottoms blanket most of the lake, and that mud is full of benthic organisms like midge larvae and fingernail clams. So the perch root and grub for the most abundant food, and fishermen catch them over these bottoms.

Still, perch will take whatever is available with the least amount of effort. Some perch may be jammed full of zebra mussels during that stage when young mussels are free-floating, while others are filled with spiny water fleas. Perch love minnows and if these are abundant on mixed sand and gravel bottom in one lake or another, they'll forage heavily over such bottoms. Or browse among rocks for small crayfish and caddis-fly larvae.

If you're deadly serious about perch fishing, check out a library book or two on invertebrate zoology or aquatic biology, and take a few minutes to become familiar with some of the most common aquatic creatures that show up in the perch's diet. Then, check a stomach or two to see what's the current fare.

If it's crayfish, caddis flies and other rock lovers, you've a solid clue that you should head for the rocks. If it's the small, red worms or midge larvae, then look for mud. But, it's rare that you have to go to such lengths. Most days a little searching, a little drifting or looking for boat concentrations will be all it takes. Perch normally aren't hard to find.

Fish Structure

All sorts of lakes, from huge Lake Michigan to small Ohio and New Jersey lakes and reservoirs with mostly flat, featureless, bowl-shaped bottoms, hold perch. So, if there's a rule for fishing any lake, it's that perch will gather on or near underwater obstructions of rock, gravel, weedbeds or man-made objects whenever possible.

When an angler is faced with big, featureless water such as this, drifting with a Lindy rig is a good tactic that can produce catches when the situation seems fairly hopeless.

Finding And Catching Perch

And, they can be either shallow or deep, depending on time of day or season. If there's no underwater structure, they'll either travel aimlessly over the bottom in loose schools and be found almost anywhere at all, or break up into individuals or small pods and still roam with no particular plan.

Check out known or found obstructions, and if they're not schooling around those obstructions, drift or move with bottom-bumping trolling rigs with line bait until something turns up. Fish that spot until nothing more happens, then move again. Getting the picture?

Don't be afraid to experiment and change tactics, either. Sometimes drifting along with a small spinner will produce better results on scattered schools or individual fish. Sometimes drifting and casting such bottom-bumpers as jigs will produce. Sometimes even trolling will help find fish, especially if using such tactics as reverse trolling with an electric motor to keep speed at a crawl on windy days. Needless to say, topo maps that show a lake's bottom help, and a fish locator will raise your odds, too. But with or without such aids, perch can be found. Eventually.

Anglers who don't own boats and have no friends that do can either rent a boat and motor for a day or half day at many marinas, or try their luck on a charter or head boat at large lakes, such as the Great Lakes. On a charter craft, usually four to six anglers will share expenses, and be taken out by a guide who will take them to waters he knows well.

Charter boats are usually successful at bringing back a good catch, since they're out there day after day, know where the fish are and want you to do well for that valuable word of mouth advertising to friends.

Head boats charge by the head, usually somewhere between $15 and $25 per person, and these big craft will take out crowds of people to fish over productive reefs and flats. They're successful, too, most days and far less expensive, but there's at least some hassle involved. With dozens of lines in the water, and some anglers each trip that are totally inexperienced, there'll be tangles to unravel, and on rare occasions, others pushing in close to fishermen making a good catch. But head boats can be fun, with lots of good companionship and a cooler filled with fish at day's end. Some perch hunters do their fishing no other way.

Proper Rigs And Tackle

Knowing something about a favorite fish's life and loves is important, but understanding how to find and catch some is important, too. When it comes to perch fishing, having the right tackle ranks high. But, since perch aren't particularly wary panfish, nothing near the class of a brown trout rising to terrestrials, they can be caught on a vast variety of rigs and tackle.

In days of yore, old time semi-commercial fishermen took them from piers using a pulley arrangement for a long trotline holding dozens of hooks. The hooks were baited, the line run out to deep water, and retrieved every half hour or so for removing fish and rebaiting.

Less commercial early-day anglers routinely fished for perch with rods bearing 8 to 10 hooks near line's end, to catch as many as possible in a short time. Perch have been taken on cane poles with black nylon cord, on rusty old closed-face reels or new ones, on sophisticated, super modern graphite rods with a near computer for a reel, even on hand lines and, doubtless, bent safety pins. Again, they're not picky, and unless hard fished, nor particularly cautious about what they eat.

But, naturally, there's a happy medium for a perch rod and reel combination, and for rods the key words are "short and sensitive."

Jigging with Doll Flies

Two leadhead jigs with marabou dressing, also known as doll flies, tied in a tandem rig manner, can be dynamite particularly for pier fishermen jigging along the pier edges.

Boat anglers fishing with a half dozen or more friends need short rods to prevent hooking partners as well as fish. They're not as important to pier fishermen, but even here it can get crowded on busy weekends, and a short rod is safer and just as effective.

A rod should be sensitive, too, which means graphite or some combination of graphite and other materials. Perch bite with vigor on occasion, but often they suck on a minnow gently, and a vague tap or slight pull is an angler's only indication of a hit. It's easy to miss a bite altogether with a billiard-cue rod.

Line? Nothing special needed here, either. Many anglers, perhaps most, fish these finned morsels with 10- to 12- pound test line, and that's fine. In clear-water lakes throughout the North, it might be better to drop to 6 or even 4, if they're moderately spooky. But any good monofilament in a wide weight range will do the job, and do it well.

Plenty of perch hunters argue lazily, even heatedly, over what constitutes the best terminal gear for a morning of productive fishing, and there are a number of types to choose from, some better suited for a given situation than others. But, in most places, whether it be a New Jersey pond or Lake Erie, the favorites are spreaders and tandem hook rigs.

Standard Rigs

A spreader is basically a pair of wire arms that hang down well to the side of a centrally placed swivel. Each arm has a loop from which dangles a 6-inch or so piece of monofilament and a hook, and in the center directly below the swivel is a third piece of line with a sinker attached. The sinker line is a bit longer than the monofilament lines that hold the hooks, so that when the lead touches bottom, the hooks and their bait are a few inches off the bottom. With some rigs, the sinker line may be shorter than the hook lines so anglers should drop the rig all the way to the bottom, then reel up a few turns to properly place the bait just a few inches above the bottom.

Spreaders vary a bit in other ways, with some having gold or red beads as an attractant, gold hooks and perhaps other modifications. But whatever their variations, the rigs have accounted for millions of perch. If they have a weakness, it's that fish must pull the wire down several inches to register a bite. With a vigorous hit, that's no problem, but those that hit very gently can steal the

Using Spreader Rigs For Perch

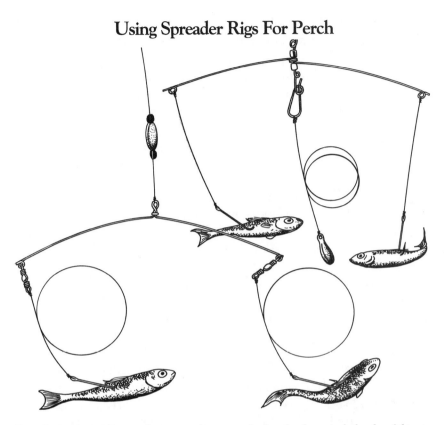

Spreader rigs for catching perch are a popular approach where legal, particularly when fishing in the Great Lakes that hold concentrations of perch. Two variations are shown here.

angler's bait without the angler knowing it.

A slightly better rig is the tandem hook rig. Basically, this one has a sinker of perhaps half an ounce at line's end, the first hook a few inches above on a short side line, and 6 to 8 inches above that another hook on a second side line. Why is it better? Because the two hooks spaced one above the other cover more vertical territory, and pick up fish swimming a foot or so above the rocks as well as those nearly on bottom. Also, the hooks dangle nearly straight down, so any pull, however gentle, is going to register.

Many anglers make their own tandem hook rigs, simply cutting a piece of monofilament from line's end, adding a hook and tying it in the appropriate position above the sinker. Other anglers purchase snelled hooks which are already attached to a piece of monofilament with a loop on the opposite end. It's quick and easy to tie these snelled hooks at proper distances up a line, using as many as three if state law permits.

Hooks, snelled or plain, will vary with an angler's situation. When fishing for jumbo perch with large minnows, a No. 4 hook is a good choice. For average fish on average bait, a smaller, No. 6 works best, and for situations where an angler can find only small minnows, a No. 8 is less noticeable and will take just as many perch. Some anglers hook a single barb of a small treble hook into a minnow's tail, leaving the other two points exposed.

Rigs For Finding Fish

For searching out schools on broad, featureless water, the most popular rig consists of a trolling slip-sinker above a swivel with roughly 18 inches of leader tied to the trailing hooks. This rig is dropped to the bottom, and the angler drifts slowly along waiting for something to happen. On an open-faced reel, the bail should be kept open and line held lightly with a finger. With closed-faced reels, keep a finger hard on the release. When a bite comes, give slack line for a count of 10, then tighten up and when weight is felt, strike!

Trolling rigs for live bait offer a good way to cover plenty of territory, find schools, and drift over them repeatedly. Commercial trolling rigs are available with small, brightly-colored foam floats a few inches above the hook, both to raise baits farther off bottom and to act as an attractant. Use them whenever possible when drift fishing.

There are plenty of variations on this fish-finder rig. Anglers can make their own slip sinker and hook combinations, of course, and some trade the foam floats for a small, very light, silver or gold spinner to add flash and draw fish.

Other Trolling Rigs For Perch

The old-time trolling standard was, and in many places still is, a three-way swivel with a short line and sinker of whatever size it takes to reach and hold bottom attached to one of the swivels. The angler's line is tied to a second swivel, and the third one normally holds 2 to 3 feet of monofilament and a hook with worm or minnow. Frequently, a small spinner is used, too, as an attractor, and often the live bait is replaced with a fast wiggling little crankbait.

Downriggers or wire lines are used more to troll for such

Tandem Hook Rig

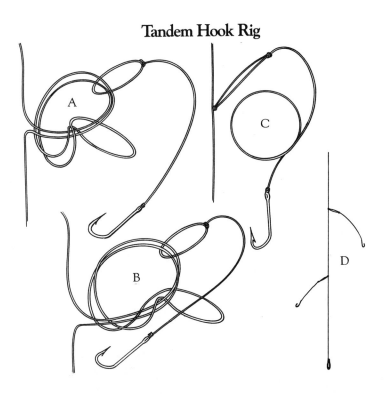

Here's a quick way of setting up a tandem hook rig, using leadered snell hooks. The line is looped through the loop on the leader in A and the hook brought through the loop in the line in B. Pull tight to keep hook in place on the line. Another hook and walking sinker is added below.

gamefish as salmon and walleye, but both will produce for larger perch, so long as downrigger releases are set very lightly. The only important requirement is to keep that bait near bottom, adjusting weight and boat speed until the right combination is found. Also, keep baits traveling as slow as humanly possible. Perch will some-times chase a fast-moving morsel until they catch it, but not often.

Other Perch Offerings

Many a nice perch has been caught off piers and boat docks, especially where water is fairly deep and there's some weedbed cover around. Spreaders or tandem-hook rigs work fine here, and are the usual choice. But an angler walking a pier, with little com-petition from other anglers, can often cover more territory and take more fish using very small jigs. In states where two hooks can

Finding And Catching Perch

These fish were taken on a spreader rig (see diagram on page 189) which is a popular rig among Great Lakes perch fishermen. Taking a double can really add excitement to your day's fishing.

be used on the same line, tie one small white jig about a foot above the first hook. The jigs, sometimes called doll flies, can have twister tails, or soft, "breathing" maribou or other materials. Some tip them with a bit of minnow or worm, but it isn't necessary.

Finally, don't forget jigging spoons. These are finger-shaped, solid-metal spoons with a single or treble hook below and usually a small colored blade to add flutter. Anglers bait them with a minnow or two, lower to the bottom, and jig up and down. They can be productive offerings for larger perch.

Using Live Baits

Yellow perch eat a wide variety of foods, and anglers can seek them with an equally wide variety of baits. But, the most popular has got to be live minnows. Perch will bite on dead minnows, too, when they're feeding avidly, and many are caught on frozen bait left over from a previous trip. They'll even take heads of minnows or half a bait fish when hunger is upon them. But there's no question that lively offerings that swim and struggle vigorously in the strike zone are better.

Perch most often grab a minnow by its head. When they take a lip or eye-hooked bait, they will sometimes have the barb embedded deeply in their throat. This rarely happens with back-hooked minnows, but it's far easier for a perch to snatch a back-hooked minnow without taking the hook at all.

Worms are a second favorite live bait that will take nearly as many perch as minnows in most situations. In fact, some old timers use them exclusively, simply because they're easier to keep and care for than minnows.

There are yet other baits occasionally used for perch. Mayfly larvae are favorites wherever found, and waxworms are both easy to buy in bait shops, and attractive to perch, especially when fished on bright and shiny miniature teardrop spoons. Mealworms have been used now and again, as have tiny crayfish, small grasshoppers and crickets, goldenrod galls and leeches. Perch have taken them all, at one time or another, but minnows are still the top bait, with worms a close second.

14

Special Situations For Perch

There are many ways to catch perch, and at one time or another, anglers have used most of them. In addition to hook and line, perch have been taken in nets or by spearing, and American Indians once trapped hundreds at a time in fences or weirs made from willows. These days, nearly all yellow perch are caught by fishermen either working from the bank or in a boat, but the two techniques require sometimes radically different methods.

Pier Fishing
More people fish perch from dry land on the Great Lakes than water, simply because it's much easier and more economical than launching a boat, renting one or heading out on a charter. What better way to spend a morning or a whole day than loafing along some well-paved fishing pier with friendly companions, a soft seat and lapping waves to soothe the soul? Pier fishermen find spots to try their luck along the entire Great Lakes, and at many of the larger and medium-sized lakes in perch country. Even small lakes usually have a few boat docks or small piers to fish from. Plenty of places to seek perch.

Most perch hunters hike out onto a promising pier, find a spot not too close to the next angler, set up shop and start fishing. On lots of days, that's all it takes. Bait a spreader or two hooks above a sinker rig with minnows, drop it straight down to bottom, then sit back and enjoy life while waiting for that rod tip to bounce, signal-

Pier fishermen rely heavily upon small jigs for nailing perch that hang around piers. Baitfish and other food usually are concentrated around the pier's uprights, attracting the perch.

Special Situations For Perch

ing that there is a finny customer on the line below.

But along many smaller piers, or at certain seasons of the year, this method can produce poorly, even not at all. So, it pays to know a few techniques that will help build a catch of dinner makings. For openers, there are two top times to fish most piers, early spring and late fall. Perch are caught all summer from some piers, especially those that end in deep water, but these are the two best seasons for taking perch.

In early spring, the fish are coming in to spawn, and they might be holding in just a few feet of water, moving restlessly here and there, swarming against obstructing piers, and turning to swim up or down their length. If the pier borders a large creek or river, so much the better, but either way, pier anglers (dressed warmly) can take good catches of good-sized fish by doing little more than fishing straight down, or giving their baits just a tiny lob to get them a few feet out.

And, it usually doesn't matter much where on the pier the angler sits, either. Setting up shop near shore will often produce just as well as setting up at the end of the pier, since schools are roaming freely in and out. In fact, it's not unusual to sit on a pier and *watch* a school coming your way. First, a few anglers somewhere along the line suddenly start catching fish, to the envious interest of their fellows.

They'll pull in perch after perch for a few minutes, then action slows and suddenly a few folk closer to you start reaching for rods. Eventually people 10 feet away are hoisting flopping perch onto the pier, then you see your own rod tips drop, and brace for action. Perching is like that on early spring piers, hit or miss, fast or slow, depending on where the schools move.

Fall action on the big piers is little different. The fish will be deeper, which means it's wise to walk out a little farther, but the rapidly cooling water triggers perch appetites. So, schools are moving, foraging, swinging this way and that, and sooner or later they'll come in your direction.

Tactics For Tough Times

It's in the balmy days of late spring, summer and early fall that fishing can get tough on piers, large or small, wherever an angler tries his luck. But on many of these piers, perch can still be had. And one thing to keep in mind now is that with only a few exceptions like wind and weather (perhaps Solunar Periods if you agree with them), the top action will be early and late.

Many a perch seeker has walked out on his chosen pier at first light, hammered them until 9 a.m. or so, then had action slack off. Walking back to his car or pickup with a fine catch, he's constantly stopped by others heading out, and they hurry on with eager feet, hoping to glean a share of this man's success. Frequently, they don't. There may be days when best action will be from late morning through early afternoon, but not many.

Another basic fact over the summer months is that on the average pier, the farther out you walk, the better you'll do. Perch are in deeper water now, and the end of the pier abuts the deepest water reachable by a bait and sinker. It can be a long hike, weighted down with gear and bait, but every step is likely to be worth it.

Finally, there are going to be sections of any pier that are consistently better than others, and anglers who visit a given structure frequently should take careful note of whose rod tip bounces the most often. It might happen that one stretch of pier will have pure mud beneath, something that perch avoid. Another will have gravel and small boulders, great hiding spots for insect larvae, minnows and crayfish.

Perch will forage here repeatedly, and return again and again, drawn by an abundance of food items. Another stretch may be mixed sand and gravel, spots that perch will check out and cross, but seldom linger long. Watch others, and then next trip try those spots where you witnessed success.

On any pier, it pays to move that bait as much as possible, both vertically and horizontally. If action is good straight down, stick to it, but if results are skimpy, try casting out just a few yards, then a few yards more. Cast slightly left and slightly right, too, if other anglers aren't too close. Fish a fan-shaped pattern, and move baits at least every 10 minutes until a school is located. There could be 200 fish feeding avidly just 20 yards from your sitting spot, but if you're not fishing there . . .

Move yourself, too. Some anglers are just too lazy to pick up gear and head farther out, farther in, or to a pier's other side, even if results are better there. Some anglers design little carry-alls or pull-alongs on wheels that allow them to change locations almost instantly, and that's a good idea. Even without such aids, your catch will definitely be better if you're willing to try more than one spot along a pier's length.

And, finally, give that bait plenty of action. Perch are predators, their eyes attuned to movement of any kind that indicated an unwary food item. Lively minnows will do the job for you, but if they're dead or nearly so, which can happen after a few hours fishing, it's wise to have a few inches of slack in the line, and reach over occasionally to twitch it, causing minnows to rise and fall. Twitch them every 10 to 15 seconds if you can stand it, and don't be surprised if bites come just shortly after those twitches.

Other Baits

As pointed out before, most perch fishermen seek their dinner with minnows, and usually they work fine. But there'll be cases when the water swarms with minnows, and every perch caught has a bulging belly and perhaps a tail or two sticking out of its mouth. Trying to feed a perch minnows then is like asking a man stuffed with potatoes if he's like another potato. He might eat it, but he's not too interested. At times like these, hauling along some worms, a few mayfly larvae, a small leech or two and waxworms can make

Pier Fishing Techniques

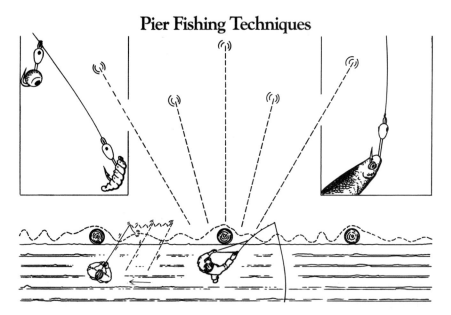

Two effective ways of finding perch and improving your catch ratio is through fan casting and jigging basically parallel to the edge of the pier. Be sure to work thoroughly around pilings.

In early spring, it can be a heyday for dock and pier fishermen as the perch move into the shallower water to spawn. The action will be fast enough that the chill in the air isn't noticed.

a major difference. A man stuffed with potatoes can always find a little room for a steak, and, usually, perch can find room for these favorite baits.

Artificial Offerings

Naturally, there are refinements to bait fishing, and one is to switch, during slack periods, to artificial offerings. Few people do, but those who use plastic and metal with authority often take perch when others don't. Like to hear about a near lethal method of perching along piers that have few or no other people? It's a simple tactic.

Tie a white jig, one with either a tiny, rippling soft-plastic tail or a soft marabou to your line, leaving a 2-foot tag end on the line. Jigs of $^1/_{32}$ to $^1/_{16}$ ounce are perfect. Then, tie another jig to the end

Special Situations For Perch

of the line, so that the lures are about a foot apart. Be sure your state allows two hooks on one line.

Drop the pair to bottom, reel up until the bottom lure is just inches above the substrate, then walk slowly up and down the pier keeping that rod tip moving and the lures hopping slowly and gently up and down. Work them around every piling, move the jigs out a few feet then in, but keep them hopping slowly. Every perch around is likely to try his luck on one or the other, and perch will be joined by rock bass, sunfish, crappie, channel cats and even northern pike where they're found. In fact, one angler fishing in a Lake Michigan pier actually saw a whopper carp swim in and suck a white jig right up his bugle snoot. Landed after a 10-minute fight, the fish weighed nearly 15 pounds!

There are other ways to fish jigs. In lakes with piers or boat docks and plenty of vegetation, it's not unusual to see someone casting single jigs in all directions, though concentrating on deeper water and territory near or between weedbeds. They'll use various colors including white, brown, black, even chartreuse and blue, switching occasionally until they find what interests the waiting perch most.

It's a slow business, but productive when a pier-walking angler wants a few fish for lunch, but doesn't want to go to the trouble of assembling equipment and finding bait. Just cast the little offering with your lightest rod and line, let it sink to bottom, and crow-hop it back with plenty of tip action to make the jig twitch and jerk like a live thing. If perch are around and hungry, they'll hammer such baits steadily.

Don't forget spinners and crankbaits, either. When perch are shallow in early spring and late fall, or foraging at dusk and dawn around weedbeds in some shallow little lake, they'll readily take spinners, especially those light-colored or white, and fished as slowly and as deep as possible. Lead-bodied spinners seem to work best for this, since varying the retrieve will see the spinner returning at depths greater than most light spinners can handle.

Crankbaits work, too, especially for larger perch, but they should dive fast, stay deep and be small. Slender, little minnow plugs are good, as are miniature crankbaits that resemble crayfish or minnows. Fish them deep as possible, even adding a rubber-core sinker or split shot farther up the line if necessary, and fish them at slow to moderate speeds. They'll work in a pinch.

Boat Fishing: Taking It To The Perch

Boat fishermen consistently do better than pier anglers, simply because they can move around over a large area and find fish, rather than waiting for schools to come to them. But even here, an angler can score poorly, and a major reason is that too many fishermen feel that one spot is as good as another.

So they head out, drop anchor at random, and sit there all morning, even all day. Sometimes such uninformed anglers get lucky and make a fine catch. More often, they head home with few or no perch, and a poor opinion of fishing in general.

Unquestionably, the easiest way to catch a mess of perch from a boat is to head out and look for concentrations of other boats. In the Great Lakes and on many large to medium-sized waters, an angler will find some fish, another will see him catching them and anchor near his boat, then another comes, and another. Finally, there might be 50 craft or more fishing over a small area, and more coming from all directions to join in the largess.

Usually, such boat concentrations will be over a favorable bottom where perch are finding food. And quite often, as one school moves out, another moves in, so that spot may provide off-and-on action all day as schools prowl from one place to another. But, it's important to carry binoculars, or at least watch other boats keenly when you're planning to set up with such clusters. It can happen that the first boats found a small school which eventually left, and the craft are sitting there stubbornly hoping another will come by. If rods aren't lifting and fish flashing at least occasionally as they're hoisted aboard, you might best search elsewhere.

Anglers planning to find their own fish, or fishing lakes that lack any concentration of perch boats should remember, again, that early spring fish will be shallow; late spring, summer and early fall fish will tend to be at least reasonably deep, and late fall fish shallower than summer ones, sometimes substantially less.

So, at any given season, head for where you think they might be, perhaps pinning down several locations from bait shop operators, or the words of fellow anglers. Then, if the boat has a depthfinder, drift or motor slowly over an area until a school is spotted below. At this point, a marker can be tossed over, the boat maneuvered upwind, and an anchor dropped gently with enough line to get the craft quietly over that school. If they prove to be perch, fish away perhaps adding a bow anchor to keep the boat

These boat anglers were well on their way to a limit of perch concentrated around a submerged reef. If the first is large, the remaining fish will be, too.

from swinging. If some other species, lift anchor and travel until another school is seen.

Markers, incidentally, are important tools on large, featureless lakes with very few islands or other reference points. They can be fancy little floating flags purchased at a marina or sporting goods store, or just a piece of colored wood with enough string wrapped around it to reach bottom, and a 2- to 4- ounce sinker at line's end to hold the marker in place. Tossed out, the sinker plummets to the bottom, causing the wood to spin and the line to unwind, and gives a precise visual reference to the school's location. Be sure to pull your marker at the end of the day.

Wind Drifting

Anglers who don't have a depthfinder, and many of those with smaller craft won't, can still find perch by wind drifting. It's limited to winds of just a few knots, but such days happen often, and when they do, just drop a tandem-hook rig with a good bottom walker sinker, and drift with the wind. You'll catch fish if they're down there and you can anchor over the spot, and if it was only a straggler, continue drifting. Never sit and fish endlessly in one spot when action is scant or nonexistent.

If winds are too strong to drift slowly, try a sea anchor if you have one to slow the boat's pace. Otherwise, use heavier walking sinkers to keep the bait bumping bottom, and drift until a perch strikes, and again anchor. When winds are quite strong, your only choice will be to anchor for five to 10 minutes in each spot. If perch are present, several should be taken within that time span, and fishing will likely be productive there. If not, hoist the anchor and move on.

Do keep in mind that hard-rock bottom or at least sand and gravel beat mud, and fishing with a sinker will soon tell any angler with sensitivity in their fingers that the sinker is bumping rocks or conversely, sinking into soft muck. If rocks are a possibility, you'll definitely want to be using one of the snagless sinkers such as the lead wire in surgical tubing which will release, if snagged.

Weather Factors

There will inevitably be days when the fish just don't bite, even though you might see schools below on a fish locator, or hear anglers say, "Man, they were sure hitting here yesterday. You

You can pick a spot and anchor, and then pull anchor and move to another spot, but drift fishing normally will pay off much better when you're trying to fill your cooler with tasty perch.

should have been here then." And weather can be a major factor.

Along Lake Erie, for example, many fishermen won't go out during an east or northeast wind because perch bite poorly when winds blow from these directions. In fact, it's not unusual to be fishing and doing well, then have winds shift to the east and action slack off to almost nothing. There are exceptions, of course, and times when for other reasons they'll hit on an east wind, but a professor from Ohio State University did a study on the problem, and came up with an interesting theory.

He believed that since prevailing winds are from the west and south, less often from the north, and rarely from the east, that winds from this latter direction set up alien water currents that the fish recognize as *wrong* and that puts them off their feed. He also thought that warm south winds brought good, though fast hatches of aquatic insects, stimulating sudden feeding binges, while less warm, west winds caused slow, steady hatches and feeding behavior that might last for hours. North winds are usually cold, and that can prevent hatches and cause slow fishing, while again insects consider east winds wrong, and may not hatch at all.

The fact remains, however, that there's still a lot to be learned about the effects of weather and the elements on fishing, particularly as far as perch are concerned. But that doesn't prevent an angler from using those so-called "barren" times on the water to do some serious experimentation. The challenge of finding and enticing fish to bite can be as much fun as the actual catch.

Other Panfish

15

White Bass And Yellow Bass

Considering their sporty aggressiveness and prolific numbers, white bass and yellow bass would seem to demand much more respect than they usually get. Nevertheless, the outdoor press pays little attention to these fish, and anglers appear more intent on catching other more renowned species.

Obscurity can't efface the first-class sporting qualities of these spunky gamefish, though. Both produce a wealth of entertainment value. Their small size belies their militant fighting ability, and when glamour fish get lockjaw, white and yellow bass can turn a potentially dismal fishing trip into a delightful one.

White and yellow bass are members of the temperate bass family, which also includes the striped bass. Because they look alike and are occasionally found together, they are sometimes confused. Separate the two by looking at the dorsal fins. On yellow bass, the fins are slightly connected by a thin membrane; the fins are separate on white bass. Both species have distinct dark side stripes, but on yellow bass the lines are broken and offset above the anal fin. Yellow bass are usually brassy yellow in color while whites are usually more silver.

It would take volumes to cover all the facets of fishing for these linesides, but the following thumbnail sketches will give you the basic information needed to catch whites and yellows throughout the year. Whites and yellows are easy to find and provide excitement that's difficult to duplicate with other gamefish.

When you find white bass or yellow bass, you often find them by the hundreds and catches like these are common. Some of the best times are during the late summer "jumps".

White Bass And Yellow Bass

White Bass: The Year-Round Fish

White bass, also known as sand bass or silver bass, inhabit portions of at least 30 states. Their original range encompassed river systems in the Mississippi and Ohio valleys and the Great Lakes, but today, due to widespread introductions, they are available throughout much of the central and eastern United States. The world record, a 5-pound, 14-ounce fish, came from Kerr Lake, North Carolina, in 1986.

The white bass (Morone chrysops) was once considered rather inconsequential. But when the age of large impoundments began, there was newfound interest in this sporty panfish. Whites could quickly populate open-water habitat seldom used by black bass, thus offering additional fishing opportunities without competing with other popular gamefish. They also provided a means of controlling prolific shad populations, since these forage fish constitute their primary prey.

Many white bass entered lakes naturally from their native streams, but they were also stocked to take advantage of their many fine sporting qualities. Whites run in schools and offer fish-a-minute action. They are spirited fighters, superb table fare, amazingly prolific and fairly easy to catch.

White bass seldom disappoint, especially if you scale down your tackle to better suit the game. A 2-pounder is a nice fish, and 3-pounders are bragging size in most waters. Since whites favor open water with few obstructions, they're perfect quarry for ultra-light tackle.

Spinning or spincasting gear with 4- to 8-pound test line is appropriate for most white bass situations. Even a 1-pound white is a worthy opponent on such gear, and the 3-pounders often encountered put up an exciting battle on ultra-light tackle. Small minnows, jigs, streamers, shad- or minnow-imitation plugs and spoons are effective enticements during any season.

One of the best times to fish for white bass is when they leave large rivers and lakes on tributary spawning runs. In some regions, anglers crowd the banks of productive feeder streams to get in on the action. Everyone has loads of fun, and success in some areas is measured by the number of five-gallon buckets that are filled with fish destined for the frying pan.

Timing of the spawning runs varies widely throughout the fish's range, but checking water temperature can help you pin-

White Bass

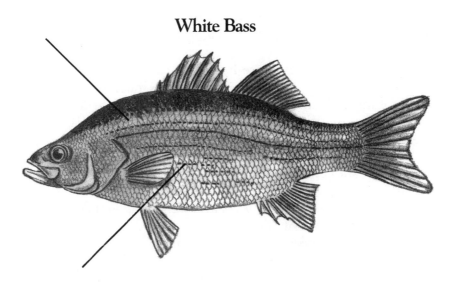

White bass have silvery sides marked by unbroken black stripes above the lateral line. Below the lateral line the strips are faint, while yellow bass have distinct stripes below this line.

point this activity. Readings of 53 to 57 degrees trigger the white's instinctive upstream migration.

When spawning ends, white bass begin cruising open lake water. They rise in schools and slash into small baitfish, making a great surface commotion. This activity typically follows the availability of meal-size shad, and peaks in late summer when young-of-the-year shad have reached about 2 inches in length.

Anglers move close to cast along the edges of the surfacing white bass schools, trying not to alarm the fish. Fish after fish may be caught for several minutes; then the school submerges, only to come up again, perhaps nearby, perhaps at a distance. There's another rush and more action. This is called "jump fishing" and is a very popular fishing method.

Summer whites are active at night. Anglers hang lanterns from their boats or drop floating lights on the water to attract baitfish. Whites are attracted to the baitfish; a bait is dropped into the schooling shad and minnows. Waiting white bass hit the bait hard, and as fast as you can get another down to them.

When whites aren't schooling on top, locate them with depth sounders and catch them by jigging spoons, bucktail jigs or plastic grubs. Swift, churning waters below dams also hold concentrations. Many anglers catch these tailwater fish by tightlining from the bank or wading the shallows, being sure to stay a safe distance from the dam.

Autumn challenges white bass anglers. Fish are scattered at this time, and the key to success is covering as much water as possible. Trolling shad-imitation lures that cover multiple depths produces good results. Single catches are usual, with "hit and run" tactics being most effective.

Deep jigging is a fast way to put winter whites in a livewell. Deep-water sunken islands, bars, bridge pilings and points are excellent locations. When sonar indicates fish below, lower a spoon, jig or minnow to the proper level and work it up and down. This produces many "instant" limits.

One fact that makes white bass fishing such fun is that any angling technique can be successfully applied to catching them. From tightlining on the bottom with weighted minnows to topwater popping with a fly rod and all techniques in between, there's a place in the white bass angler's arsenal for it all. Finding a school of white bass is a good definition of entertainment.

Broken or "offset" dark stripes above the anal fin help identify this nice catch as yellow bass. Yellow bass are prolific but may be abundant in one lake and nonexistent in the next.

White bass prefer open waters and are often caught in the middle of a lake or stream, far from any noticeable cover. When you find them, be ready for some fast-paced fishing.

White Bass And Yellow Bass

When you set the hook with ultra-light tackle on a white bass like this, get ready for a real battle. The angler caught this dandy on a Little George tailspin.

Yellow Bass: The Bantam Brawler

On many waters, yellow bass are considered more of a small-sized nuisance than a sportfish. But don't write them off just because they're small. If you're looking for some fast-paced fun on light tackle, these scrappy little fighters can keep you happy for hours on end. On some waters, it's not uncommon for an angler to catch 100 or more a day.

Barfish, stripe, gold bass, yellowjack, streak and yellow perch are common nicknames for the yellow bass (Morone mississippiensis). The species is confined primarily to the central Mississippi Valley, where it inhabits quiet pools and backwaters of large rivers, reservoirs and natural lakes. It is scattered in abundance. A lake here, a river there, offers good yellow bass fishing, but many others in the same area may not.

Most yellow bass weigh only a few ounces, and even record-size fish are barely over 2 pounds. There are rumors of 5-pounders from Louisiana waters, but a 2-pound, 4-ounce yellow bass caught in Lake Monroe, Indiana, in 1977 is the largest catch that has been officially documented.

Claims that yellow bass are always caught in deep water near the bottom are simply hearsay. It's true that yellow bass rarely exhibit the surface-feeding sprees for which white bass are famous, but studies indicate they usually feed on small crustaceans, insects and fish at mid-depth or near the surface. Open water is a common haunt, but they frequent areas of shallow cover, too, and are often caught around stumps, weedbeds, riprap, cypress knees, and brush.

Yellow bass readily take a wide variety of baits. Perhaps the best is a small leadhead jig. Worms, crickets and small minnows are also relished, and fly fishing with small streamers or wet flies is very effective.

Use ultra-light tackle for maximum enjoyment. Yellow bass fight much like the various sunfishes, and when you're bringing one in on a whippy spinning rod or jigging pole, its scrappy, cut-and-run fighting style may convince you you've hooked a much larger fish.

Yellow bass can be caught year-round using the same tactics employed for white bass. But, during most of the year, trolling or drift fishing with small jigs is the best method for locating loose schools. Start by using a variety of jigs rigged at different depths. For instance, if you are using six poles, set two jigs two feet deep, two at four feet, and two at six feet. Use various sizes and colors — some $1/16$-ounce, some $1/32$, some black, some yellow, some silver. This allows you to test different baits and depths until a preference is established. Once you ascertain that yellow bass favor a certain depth or jig style, then rig all poles to conform to that preference.

Yellow bass may not get very big, but size isn't everything. If you've ever spent a long day on the water fishing unsuccessfully for some highly touted gamefish, you can appreciate how a few quick skirmishes with this bantam brawler can lift your sagging spirits.

16

Rock Bass
And Warmouths

Rock bass and warmouths are like carp and gars—they don't get much respect. A half-pounder is a whopper in most waters, and fishermen usually consider them little more than a freebie. It's fine if you catch one; it's fine if you don't. Despite their small size, though, rock bass and warmouths have a lot going for them. Ounce for ounce, they are among our most sporty panfish. They are extremely aggressive and will gobble up almost anything tossed in the water, including bass-sized lures almost as big as they are.

For this reason, they make excellent sport for children and other less experienced anglers. Rock bass and warmouths are widespread, plentiful, easy to catch and excellent eating when properly prepared. They give an angler the sense of having faced a challenge and won, and panfishermen who overlook these spunky little fighters are missing out on a lot of pure, old-fashioned panfishing fun.

Rock bass and warmouths belong to the sunfish family along with the black basses and true sunfishes like the bluegill. They are intermediate relatives of both, as their appearance indicates. They have a big mouth like a bass, but retain a distinctive sunfish look. They're more robust and have thicker fillets than a typical bluegill, but they're not as thick and elongated as a smallmouth bass. If you could cross a smallmouth bass and a sunfish, the result would probably resemble a rock bass or warmouth.

These two lookalikes are often confused, but savvy anglers

Jigs are a popular and quite productive artificial for catching rock bass. You can use larger jigs, even up to $^1/_8$ ounce, because these fish have large mouths for a panfish.

Rock Bass And Warmouths

should have little trouble identifying their catch. Warmouths have a rough patch of teeth on the tongue that can be detected by rubbing a forefinger over the tongue's upper surface. Rock bass have no rough tongue patch. The two can also be distinguished by counting the spines at the front of the anal fin. Warmouths usually have three anal fin spines, while rock bass typically have six. Also, dark spots on the scales form horizontal lines on the sides of rock bass, whereas the warmouth has ragged, dark, vertical bars with scattered spots in between.

Habitat provides another means of distinguishing the pair. Rock bass are fond of cool, clear, rock-bottomed streams with moderate to swift current. Warmouths, on the other hand, are usually found in oxbow lakes, sluggish delta streams and fertile man-made reservoirs where weedbeds and woody vegetation are abundant. Warmouths have more tolerance for muddy water than rock bass.

There are other differences as well. Let's take an in-depth look at these two underrated panfish.

Rock Bass: The Eager Quartet

The name "rock bass" is commonly applied to four very closely related species of panfish: the Ozark bass (Ambloplites constellatus), a native of the White River system in Arkansas and Missouri and tributaries of Missouri's Osage River; the shadow bass (Ambloplites ariommus), found throughout much of the Southeast from southern Missouri to the Florida panhandle; the Roanoke bass (Ambloplites cavifrons), native to the Roanoke, Chowtan, Tar and Neuse river drainages in Virginia and North Carolina; and the true rock bass (Ambloplites rupestris), found from southern Canada, the Dakotas and New England, south to Mississippi, Alabama and Georgia. For our purposes, we'll use the term "rock bass" interchangeably when discussing this group. Though they are scientifically distinguishable, all four look very much alike. They have a big mouth, a long chunky body, bulging blood-red eyes and splotchy markings ranging from olive and gold to black and white. The color and size of the eyes have led to the appropriate common nicknames, "redeye" and "goggle-eye."

Although the range of these fish seems to indicate unusual adaptability, they are actually quite specialized. They are sometimes found in impoundments, but they prefer cool, clear streams

The rock bass is an aggressive inhabitant of the Northeast and parts of East-Central United States.

with, as the "rock bass" name implies, plenty of rocks and gravel bars to hang out on.

Creeks and rivers strewn with boulders, gravel or rock rubble, or with bedrock or shale bottoms provide ideal habitat. Rock bass are, in fact, partial to streams suited to smallmouth bass and share many with them.

When it comes to willingness to attack a lure, few gamefish can compare with rock bass. Whether you label them gullible, aggressive, or just plain eager, redeyes are suckers for properly presented artificials. Small plugs, spinners, jigs, flies, poppers—all these and more can be used to entice these bantam brawlers.

Because rock bass have large mouths, there's no need to limit your lure selection to ultra-lights. In fact, $2^{1}/_{2}$- to $3^{1}/_{2}$-inch floating-diving minnow plugs, grubs and crayfish crankbaits are ideal for this gamefish.

If you're a bait fisherman, rock bass are your type of fish, too. They especially relish small crayfish, but small minnows, aquatic insects, worms and insect larvae like hellgrammites are also important foods. Rock bass aren't any more selective about baits than they are with artificials. Generally speaking, if it wiggles, they will take a chance with it.

Rock bass like to hang out around eddies, currents breaks and

Rock Bass And Warmouths   219 rock ledges. The angler who fishes these hotspots should have little trouble finding these feisty panfish.

Eddies, areas where a stream's current swirls in a reverse pattern contrary to the main current, create little backwaters where crayfish, minnows, hellgrammites and other rock bass forage become trapped. Rock bass aren't rocket scientists, but they are instinctively aware that eddies provide a smorgasbord of food items. Work a bait or lure through the swirl in a stop-and-go fashion, and get ready for a tussle.

Current breaks create areas of reduced water flow where rock bass can rest and feed on critters floating by. Slackwater areas around logs, stumps and fallen trees may hold an occasional fish, but true to their name, rock bass seem to prefer breaks created by large rocks. Use a bobber to float a small jig, live crayfish or other bait past big rocks. Strikes usually occur when the offering comes around the side of the rock, directly behind it, or several feet downstream where the relatively slow water borders or meets the stream's main flow.

Rock ledges adjacent deep pools are also favored rock bass sanctuaries. Here, you should present your offering deep, where

Small lures for rock bass include Rebel's Wee-Crawfish and Cat'r Crawler (left), and (right, top to bottom) Southern Pro's Li'l Hustler, Mister Twister's Curly Tail, Slater's jig and Arkie Lure's bass jig.

Warmouths are principally inhabitants of the South and Southeast, but can be found as far north as Ohio and Pennsylvania and as far west as Arizona.

bigger fish are likely to be holding. But keep the bait or lure close to the ledge. Look for anything that distinguishes a small section of the ledge from the surrounding wall—a small pocket or point, a fallen tree leaning into the water, a big boulder beneath the surface—then cast to the structure, let your bait settle to the bottom, and hop it back in with a slow, methodical retrieve. You'll probably lose plenty of tackle when fishing these areas, but you'll also catch plenty of nice redeyes.

Canoes are popular fishing crafts on most rock bass waters, but if you use one, don't move along too fast. Rock bass are school fish, and the biggest mistake many goggle-eye anglers make is catching one fish, then moving on before working the hole for additional schoolies. It's best to beach your canoe or anchor it once you've caught a fish, stopping long enough to work the area thoroughly.

The Warmouth: Small But Plentiful

The warmouth (Chaenobryttus gulosus) is a lover of swamps, bayous, sloughs, oxbow lakes and other warm, sluggish waters with dense timber, brush and weeds. It is especially common in the warm lowland waters of the southeastern United States but occurs sporadically as far west as New Mexico and as far north as Lake Erie and southeastern Minnesota. Some populations have been established from stockings in Idaho, Arizona and a few other areas west of the Rocky Mountains.

Like rock bass, the warmouth has a short, heavy body and a rather large mouth. It can be distinguished from all other panfish by the presence of teeth on the tongue. The sides usually have a brassy hue mottled with dark brown, fading to light yellow on the belly. Coloration is extremely variable, though. Swamp fish may be mottled a dark purplish-brown and at first appear to be entirely different from the golden-brown specimens that thrive in upland impoundments.

The name "warmouth" is probably derived from the "Indian warpaint" pattern of facial bars radiating backward from its reddish eyes to the margin of the gill covers. In some areas, it is still improperly called by an old name—warmouth bass. In other places, it goes by nicknames like goggle-eye, mud bass, weed bass, stumpknocker, bigmouth perch and jugmouth, among others.

Most warmouths are caught and released by anglers seeking bluegills, crappies, bass or other fish. Some folks shun them because of their small size. The typical fish is 8 inches long or shorter and weighs no more than half a pound, if that. They aren't the

Warmouth

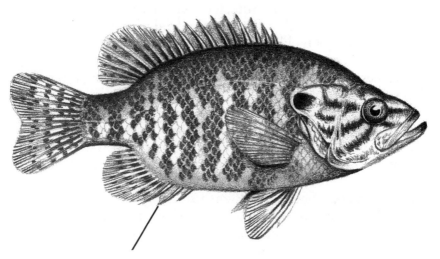

Warmouths and rock bass are mistaken for one another because they both have red eyes and mottled coloring, but the warmouth's anal fin has three spines while the rock bass' has six spines.

Tying into a scrappy warmouth brings a big smile to this angler's face. Catching warmouths on ultra-light tackle can provide a lot of fishing excitement.

Rock Bass And Warmouths

One thing about warmouths is that they're as predictable as a fish can be. Work a jig or cricket inside a flooded hollow stump or tree and prepare to take a mess like this.

most handsome member of the sunfish clan; in fact, they're down-right homely. They lack the furious spirit and determination of a hooked bluegill, and some fishermen complain they have "soft flesh with a muddy flavor."

Despite these supposed shortcomings, though, warmouths have a devoted group of followers in many areas, and for good reasons. Sure, they're small, but they're so plentiful in some waters, you could string up 50 or more before you could catch your first bass. They may not be as scrappy as bluegills, but what panfish is? Warmouths are pretty darn feisty in their own right, and on ultra-light tackle, they put up a respectable battle.

Warmouths have a big appetite and a mouth to match. They are anything but shy and will gobble up a wide assortment of lures and baits, including crickets, worms, small crayfish and minnows, insect larvae, jigs, spoons, plastic worms, spinners, flies, streamers and plugs. Poor table fare? In some poor-quality waters, perhaps, but poor taste is mostly a matter of poor preparation. Throw them on ice as soon as you catch them, and most will be good eating.

One of the nicest things about warmouths is their predictability. Find a hollowed-out cypress tree or stump in a fertile lake or stream, and chances are, if there are warmouths inhabiting those waters, there will be at least one, and maybe half a dozen hiding inside. For some reason, warmouths love dimly lit hollows, and if the hole is big enough to drop a jig, cricket or worm in, you'll soon be yanking warmouths out one after another.

Beaver lodges are another favorite hideout. Sometimes beavers build their stick homes where many of the branches are submerged, and warmouths love to hide in these dense tangles. The best way to catch them in this situation is to use a jigging pole or cane pole to lower a small leadhead jig down into the small openings of the beaver lodge. The hole need be no bigger than a half-dollar to harbor a warmouth, and though you'll lose a few jigs, this is one of the best ways to load a stringer with fat little goggle-eyes.

Mini-crankbaits are also good warmouth catchers. Use $1/12$- to $1/8$-ounce minnow or crayfish imitations fished with 2- to 4-pound test line on an ultra-light spinning or spincast combo. Cast around cypress knees, weedbed edges, stumps or other good warmouth cover, and get ready for an exciting battle with one of these spunky, big-mouthed fish. Warmouths exemplify the old saying, "Good things often come in small packages."

17

Bullheads And
Other Catfish

Growing numbers of sportfishermen have joined the ranks of loyal catfish fans in recent years. It seems that other anglers have finally realized what ardent catters have known all along, that catfish have all the qualities necessary to rank as top-flight gamefish. Flatheads and blue cats may exceed 100 pounds and fight like underwater oxen. They're muscular, mean and voracious. The channel cat isn't too shabby either—sometimes topping 50 pounds and providing the finest eating fillets you ever stuck a fork into. Like other species of catfish, it is widespread, abundant, eager to bite and can be caught using a wide variety of challenging and exciting tactics.

Bullheads: The Neglected Catfish

Despite the fishing world's newfound praise for this clan of whiskered polebenders, though, there's still one member of the catfish family that's overlooked by the vast majority of sportfishermen. The bullhead might get a little bit of begrudging admiration now and then. But, its name still isn't dropped by anglers looking for status. In fact, the bullhead—a fish that will pounce upon any offering of edibles with wild abandon, a fish that strikes hard without any pretense of caution, a fish with universal tastes that fights tenaciously and tastes superb—is entirely ignored in many areas where it is extremely common.

Why is a fish with such laudable sporting characteristics neglected by anglers? Well, the bullhead is ugly as a roadkill troll, a

Catching a nice-sized bullhead can be loads of fun, especially for young anglers who may be just getting started as fishermen. Bullheads provide good eating as well.

Bullheads And Other Catfish

fact that does nothing to help its reputation. It is slimy, it stabs careless anglers with its rapier-like fins, it grubs on the bottom like a rooting pig when looking for dinner, and it will live—quite happily—in the fish world's equivalent of a slum. A 3-pounder is considered a behemoth.

Many folks love bullheads, nevertheless. They are widely stocked, especially in small urban waters. And in some Midwestern states, they are reportedly the No. 1 ranked fish in terms of numbers taken.

Which Cat Is That?

Bullheads have some of the most colorful nicknames you've ever heard. "Horned pout" seems to be the most universal moniker, and was derived from the fish's sharp pectoral fins or "horns," and from the European word "pout" which means bigheaded fish. The nicknames "greaser" and "slick" are also widely used, and no doubt refer to the thick layer of slime that coats all bullheads. Other colloquial names include polliwog, polly, paperskin, mudcat, stinger, snapper, butterball, bullcat and bullpout.

There are four varieties of bullheads in North America, all of which grow large enough to be considered panfish. The largest is the black bullhead (Ictalurus melas), a common resident of ponds, lakes, streams and swamps from southern Canada, the Great Lakes, and the St. Lawrence River south to the Gulf of Mexico, and from Montana and New Mexico, east to the Appalachians. The all-tackle record is 8 pounds, 15 ounces, a giant taken in 1987 from Sturgis Pond in Michigan.

The brown bullhead (Ictalurus nebulosus) ranges throughout the eastern half of the United States and into southern Canada. It has been widely introduced outside its native range. It prefers moderately clear, heavily vegetated streams and lakes, and is one of the most-sought members of the bullhead clan because it averages quite large. The 5-pound, 8-ounce world record came from Georgia's Veal Pond in 1975.

The yellow bullhead (Ictalurus natalis) tends to inhabit smaller, weedier bodies of water than its cousins. It is common in areas of dense vegetation in shallow, clear bays of lakes, ponds and slow-moving streams. It, too, is widespread, ranging throughout the eastern and central United States, with many transplants elsewhere. A 4 1/2-pounder caught in Mormon Lake, Arizona, in 1989

Black Bullhead

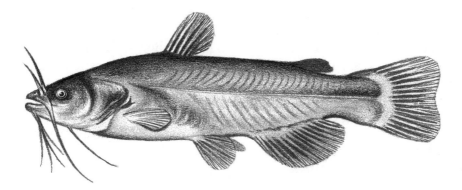

The crescent-shaped light area at the base of the black bullhead's tail separates it from yellow bullheads or brown bullheads. Bullheads' squared or slightly forked tails distinguish them from channel and blue catfish, and flathead catfish have an underbite that bullheads don't.

is the largest ever taken on rod and reel.

The flat bullhead (Ictalurus platycephalus) isn't rare, but it isn't very well known, because its range is much more restricted than that of our other bullheads. It occurs mostly in slow-water areas of large rivers in portions of Virginia, North Carolina, South Carolina and Georgia. Although this fish likes soft mud, muck or sand bottoms, it is frequently found in small- to medium-sized rock- or gravel-bottomed streams in Virginia. No records are kept, but the flat bullhead seldom exceeds one pound.

Although bullheads are generally some shade of the color in their names (black, brown or yellow—flat bullheads are yellowish), coloration varies considerably within each species and isn't a good identification characteristic. It's easy to separate the four species, though, simply by looking at the chin barbels (whiskers), fins and shape of the head.

The yellow bullhead and flat bullhead both have whitish or yellowish chin barbels, but the flat can be separated from the yellow by its flattened, sloping head and a dark blotch at the base of the dorsal fin. The brown bullhead has dark chin barbels like the black bullhead, but on browns the pectoral fin spines (on each side just behind the head) have well-developed "teeth" along the rear edge; teeth are absent or weakly developed on the black bullhead's pectoral fin spines.

Bullheads can be distinguished from channel and blue catfish by their squared or slightly forked tail; channel and blue cats have deeply forked tails. Flathead catfish have a slightly forked tail like bullheads, but bullheads lack the flathead's characteristic jutting lower jaw or "underbite."

Fishing Strategies

There is nothing difficult about catching bullheads. Anyone who has fished for channel cats can catch bullheads with essentially the same methods.

Bait choices are legion. Bullheads are the fish world's equiva-

Bullhead and catfish fishing at night can be one of the best social events around. Get the lines out, pull up a pail and the stories start to roll while you keep an eye for a bite.

Bullheads love oxbow lakes and other quiet waters. They aren't real choosy and can be taken on a variety of baits, but nothing beats a big gob of worms fished right on the bottom.

lent of barnyard hogs. There's hardly anything they won't eat. Live crayfish, minnows, nightcrawlers, shad, catalpa worms, salamanders, leeches, maggots, tadpoles or toads will do just fine. Dead stuff like chicken liver, mussels, shrimp and fish guts are on the menu as well. Weird things, too, like dog food, corn, soap, sour grain, hot dogs, marshmallows, bread, cheese and even bubblegum are acceptable. Indeed, bullheads will engulf anything remotely resembling food, so you'll probably catch one sooner or later no matter what your bait choice.

Even Henry David Thoreau noticed their indiscriminate feeding behavior. "They will take any kind of bait," he wrote, "from angleworms to a piece of tomato can, without hesitation or coquetry, and they seldom fail to swallow the hook."

While using a piece of tomato can for bait might be stretching your luck, there's no denying that these nocturnal feeders are not temperamental. Like all creatures, though, bullheads have favorite foods, and with these guys, it's worms—plain old garden hackle. Most bullhead anglers soon learn that nothing is more effective than a big wad of worms gobbed up on a hook and thrown out on the bottom. Bloody chicken liver rates a close second, but stinkbait concoctions and mussel meat are also first-rate enticements for these scavengers.

Almost any type of tackle works, even heavy gear and line. But it's best to go light if you wish to savor your rock-'em-sock-'em battles with these little cats. Four- to 8-pound line is appropriate in all but the most snag-infested waters. Hooks for bullheads range in size from No. 4 to 1/0.

Though bullheads may bite at all hours of the day, they usually feed most actively at night. You can catch them from shore or boat, but boaters have an advantage because they can better move around in search of fishing hotspots. Both types of fishermen should remember that certain stretches of a stream or lake may hold many more bullheads than other areas. Weedbed edges, river bends, channel drops, underwater humps, inundated ponds, boat docks and long points are all worth investigating. Whatever you do, don't just sit in one place without moving. Unless, of course, you're catching fish. When fishing is slow, a move of just a few yards can boost your catch considerably.

Water turbidity seems to have little to do with the catch rate. In fact, some very impressive catches are taken from the muddiest water. Bullheads tolerate high levels of turbidity better than most gamefish, and since they feed primarily by taste and smell, low visibility isn't a problem.

As a general rule, the simpler your fishing methods, the more you will enjoy bullhead fishing. Your fishing strategy can be as unencumbered as using a cane pole and small hook to dunk a worm or piece of liver in late evening. Fish on the bottom, using a split shot or a small slip sinker to carry your bait down. Or use a bobber to float the bait just slightly above the bottom. You needn't fish deep or far from shore.

Setting The Hook

Bullheads are easy to catch, but because they have tough, bony mouths, they can be difficult to hook. They also have an annoying

There's something about fishing for eager bullheads that promotes bonding between adults and kids. Perhaps it's because that's often how a youngster's fishing experience begins.

Bullheads And Other Catfish

The black bullhead is found throughout much of the United States, and is the most prevalent of the bullhead species.

habit of holding the bait in the mouth, letting the angler reel them in, then spitting it out at the last second.

To ensure that more bullheads are landed, always use extra-sharp hooks, and let the fish start moving off before you set the hook. If you're tightlining, you should feel the bullhead yank at the bait a time or two before it swims off with it. When the fish starts moving away, count five, then set the hook with a quick, upward snap of the hand. If using a bobber, simply wait until the float disappears or starts to move slowly across the water. That's usually when the fish has the bait in its mouth.

Bullheads are notorious hook swallowers, so take plenty with you. You can sometimes remove the hooks with a disgorger or long-nosed pliers. But it's usually quicker to cut the line and wait to retrieve the hooks when you clean the fish.

Whether you unhook your fish or simply snip the line, it's wise to avoid the bullhead's sharp pectoral and dorsal spines. If you do get finned, try swiping the fish's belly across the wound. The protective slime covering the bullhead's body contains something that helps neutralize the stinging sensation. If fish slime doesn't appeal to you, clear household ammonia daubed on the wound with a cotton ball has the same effect.

As with other fish, the bullhead's flavor varies according to the quality of water from which it came. Fish from muddy or polluted waters may have a strong, objectionable taste, but if you catch bullheads in clean water and put them on ice soon after being caught, they'll provide the entree for some delicious meals.

Regardless of where you catch them, always skin the fish and remove the dark red flesh along the lateral line. This rids the dressed fish of most of the unsavory flesh.

The Other Cats

Though they grow too large to qualify as panfish, the big three of catfishing—the channel cat, blue cat and flathead—are worthy of mention here, too.

The flathead catfish (Pylodictis olivaris) frequents dam tailwaters, large rivers, bayous and reservoirs throughout the Mississippi, Missouri and Ohio river basins in the central and southern U.S. It's incredibly ugly—pot-bellied, wide-headed, and beady-eyed—but what it lacks in good looks, it makes up for in size. Most will average three to 10 pounds, but 25 to 50 pounders aren't rare, and flatheads up to 139 pounds have been verified. Common nicknames include yellow cat, shovelhead cat, goujon and appaloosa cat.

The blue catfish (Ictalurus furcatus) rivals the flathead in size and can weigh 150 pounds. It's found in larger streams and reservoirs, and like the channel cat, is usually caught over bottoms of rock, gravel or sand. The native range encompasses the major rivers of the Mississippi, Ohio and Missouri basins of central and southern United States. Fulton, humpback cat, white cat and blue channel cat are commonly used colloquial names.

The channel catfish (Ictalurus punctatus) resembles the blue but seldom grows larger than 25 pounds. It's characteristic of clear, medium to large streams, but millions are produced at fish hatcheries each year and stocked in lakes and ponds throughout the country. This is our most widely distributed large catfish, with extensive introductions throughout most of the country. Regional monikers include fiddler, spotted cat, chucklehead, willow cat and blue channel.

Flatheads prefer live fish—minnows, small sunfish, or goldfish—hooked to remain lively. Blue cats are most often taken on cut or whole shad or herrings. Channel cats are like bullheads in that they'll eat practically anything and can be taken on crayfish,

Jug fishing, popular in the South, involves attaching a hook, line and sinker to the handle of a plastic jug, and baiting the rig. Then, he follows the drifting jugs until a catfish takes the bait.

Complete Angler's Library

minnows, nightcrawlers, chicken liver or many other baits.

Like bullheads, these big cats relate to structure. You may find them along drop-offs, near riprap, around rocky points, in flooded timber or beneath undercut banks. Other hotspots include quiet water behind rocks in midcurrent, deeper pools washed in stream bends, tributary mouths and around fallen trees where eddies seem to form.

Big cats usually prefer deep water during the day and shallow flats and edges at night. They prefer areas with current near their primary forage. The best fishing is usually from March through October in temperate climes.

Fishing for cats with a rod and reel is extremely popular, but many special fishing techniques are also used. Trotlining—a technique employing a heavy, 25- to 100-hook line stretched across a stream or cove—is extremely popular, especially in the South. Limblines—single lines tied to green tree limbs and baited—are good in tree-lined waters. Jug fishing involves hooks, line and weights tied to plastic bottles that serve as floats and is a good way to cover a large area with a number of baited hooks. Snagging cats in dam tailwaters using long saltwater fishing rigs and bare treble hooks is permitted in many states. Hogging involves grabbing fish with the bare hands when they are in holes or logs. You don't have to be crazy, but it helps! Of course, you should always check local fishing regulations to determine which of these methods are permitted and what restrictions may apply.

Catfish are great fighters, widely available and superb eating. If you haven't tried fishing for these powerful brutes, you should. Catfishing is one of the most enjoyable, action-packed pastimes available to NAFC anglers.

Ice Fishing
For Panfish

18

Getting Equipped For Ice Fishing

C hiseling a hole through 6 inches of blue ice, a parka-clad boy hooks a minnow to the end of his ice fishing rig—a hook, sinker and line attached to a stick he's cut from a poplar sapling. In less than a minute, he hand-lines in a tail-flapping yellow perch. This boy and thousands of other anglers annually hit the frozen lakes and river backwaters of our Ice Belt. Bluegills, crappies and perch readily feed under the ice, and there's hardly a more enjoyable way to spend a winter day than to catch a mess to be eaten later as hot, delicious fillets.

As the boy proved, anyone can afford to ice fish. But naturally, you can catch more fish with a little modern refinement. Here's a rundown of what's available for today's panfisherman.

Cutting The Hole

To chop through the ice, a sharp-ended, 5-foot ice chisel may suffice if the ice isn't too thick. The chisel (or any ice cutter) should have a sharp blade, and the blade can be greased so it doesn't rust. Holes are chopped with the chisel's straight edge on the outside of the hole and the angled edge in.

While a chisel may do, other cutters may serve an angler better. A panfishermen needs to move around a lot to locate fish. Thus, many holes may need to be cut. Hand-powered or gas- or electric-powered augers and drills make hole-cutting much less of a chore, especially when the ice reaches a foot or more thick. (If the weather's not too frigid, though, a chisel might be still handy

If you want to be an effective ice fisherman, don't get rooted to one spot. Moving around a lot helps an angler find the fish more quickly. Portable shelters make you more mobile.

Getting Equipped For Ice Fishing

when reopening and reusing prepared holes the next day.)

Augers And Drills

Hand-powered brace-and-bit augers and drills require a little bit of muscle power, but these tools cut fairly speedily and are still lightweight, commonly around the 10-pound range. The best models are ruggedly built, easily sharpened and have replaceable blades. The top models also feature handles designed to provide good leverage.

Hand augers cut easily when they are at their sharpest, so it pays to handle blades with care. A good coat of petroleum jelly or other lightweight grease repels rust when applied between uses. It's best to choose the smallest auger for the task. For most panfish, a 5-inch blade will suffice, and save you effort when drilling.

Fishing With European Style Floats

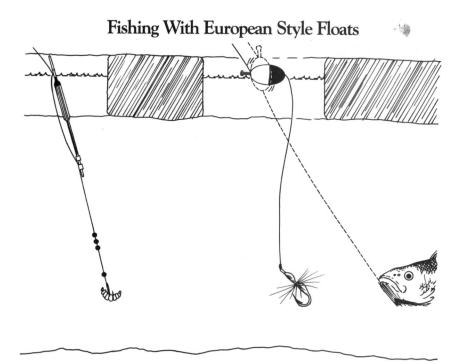

This drawing shows how two European-style floats are used in ice fishing situations. The Thill Shy Bite float (left) should be weighted so just the colored tip extends above the water while the Thill Ice'n Fly Special lays on its side until a bite pulls it upright.

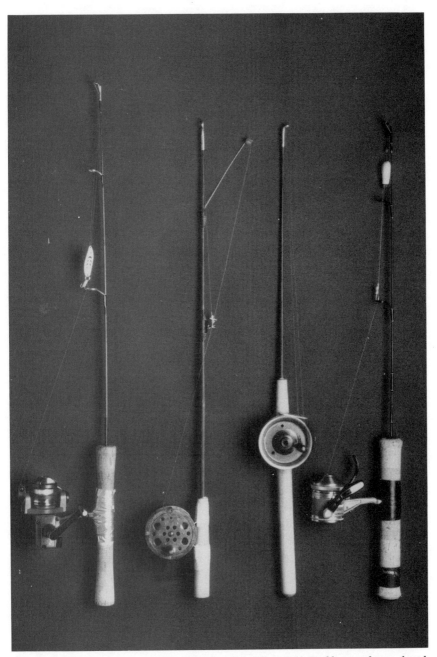

Popular jigging stick and reel combinations include (from left) Berkley graphite rod with Shimano AXUL-S spinning reel, inexpensive fiberglass rod with metal spool, home-modified fiberglass rod fitted with spring bobber and small fly reel and ultra-light graphite rod with Zebco UL4 reel.

Getting Equipped For Ice Fishing

Power Drills

Gas-powered drills with spiral blades work their way through three-foot-deep holes in a matter of seconds. These drills, commonly weighing about 25 to 30 pounds, come in different models which cut at various speeds. Gas drills range from about one and one-half to three horsepower and are fitted with 5- to 10-inch diameter drills. If the region frequently has ice that gets extra thick, the angler should buy an auger which can accommodate an extension handle for more convenient use.

Another option is the electric drill. This tool cuts a bit slower than the gas drill, maybe penetrating a couple feet of ice in about a half minute, but it's fairly lightweight—commonly weighing less than 20 pounds—and eats no gas. You can power this with a 12-volt motorcycle or auto battery.

Sleds conveniently haul your drill and other gear from car to lake, and from fishing hole to fishing hole. A lightweight children's sled can be easily pulled by hand or by snowmobile. A plastic crate or pail can be put on the sled to haul small items and can later serve as a chair and fish container. Some commercial sleds come with pop-up wind screens and storage compartments.

Panfishing Shelters

Tents, shanties and similar shelters provide protection from the cold, increase your ability to see underwater and allow you to keep your fish hidden so your spot isn't disturbed by the noise of other anglers. Shelters also help keep your fish from freezing, ensuring easier cleaning and possibly better-flavored meat.

A permanent-type fishing hut of plywood or insulated board can be used for panfishing. A large fish house with carpeted floor, stove, sleeping bunk and television offers the ultimate in comfort. These houses are best if you're located over a real hotspot. However, a portable canvas hut, tent or windbreak may serve a panfish angler better because it's more mobile.

Modern portable ice fishing shelters house one or two persons, commonly weigh 35 to 80 pounds and feature aluminum pole supports. They have built-in sled runners, and you can carry your tackle on top or inside them. They handily fold up for storage in a pickup or car trunk, and they can be set up in just a few minutes.

Of course, if the ice is plenty thick, you can drive out and pull in Mr. Panfish from the ol' pickup truck or car (which naturally

Using a power auger such as this (Magnum 3 6-inch auger from StrikeMaster) makes it much easier for a panfisherman to drill the holes required to find the fish. Mobility is the key word in finding fish and the power auger makes it much easier.

Getting Equipped For Ice Fishing

needs to be a reliable-starting vehicle or you could be caught out in the cold).

Open-Ice Clothing

Many times, fishing without any shelter results in the best catches because you can move about more freely to locate, or follow fish. But, you'll have to dress warm for this kind of fishing. Snowmobile suits and down parkas, especially those designed to keep out drafts, worn over other warm clothing, are a popular choice among ice fishermen.

Most heat loss is from the head, but a thick stocking cap and hood cures that. Feet often get cold but new multi-insulation designs in bootwear keep panfishermen comfortable, even at 50 below zero. Lined leather mitts, neoprene gloves and hand warmers keep the fingers warm. An extra pair (and a dry towel) will ensure warm hands if the first pair gets wet. A portable gas or oil heater or a lantern can provide extra heat on the ice or in a shelter.

A few other items help the open-ice angler. Ice creepers, cleats strapped on your boots, aid you in walking on slick ice, and a pair of sunglasses reduces the snow's glare. Also, an ice fisherman should bring along a compass to help find the way back to the vehicle should a snowstorm pop up.

Finding Bottom—And The Fish

Sonar units make fish-finding and fish-catching quite easy. You can quickly find the best water depths and, with the sensitivity turned up, you can see the position of your bait, and any fish that enters the water column under your hole.

You can put a simple flasher unit to use without chopping a hole; simply clear away the snow, pour water onto the ice, and put the transducer in the water. A 12-volt wet-cell battery like that used in a motorcycle is best for ice fishing as it holds plenty of power in cold weather and, at a few pounds, is not real heavy. The sonar's transducer needs to be kept level. Special brackets are available for this, or you can easily build a bracket from boards or scrap metal.

A clamp-on lead weight, a weight on an alligator clip, is another handy item, especially when fishing without an electronic depthfinder. Clamped to your hook, it lets you quickly find the lake bottom so you can adjust your float and fishing depth.

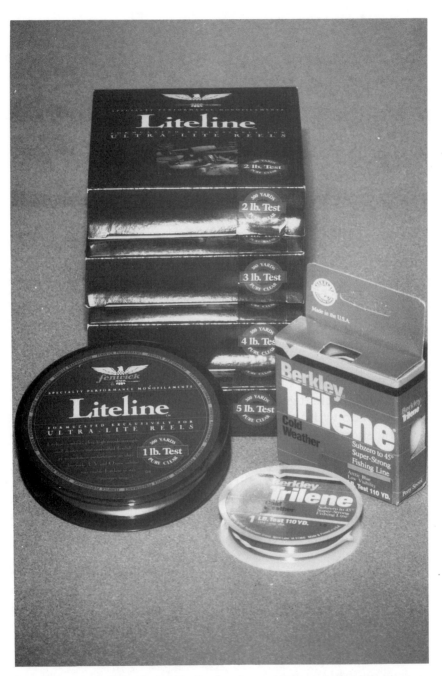

Specially designed "cold weather" fishing line from 1-pound test up in 1-pound increments are made by these and other manufacturers. Big plus is the line is less apt to kink in cold weather.

Getting Equipped For Ice Fishing

Searching With Sonar

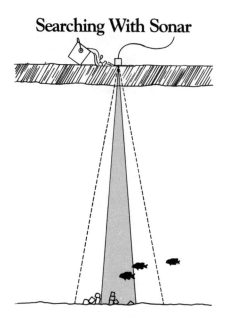

If you want to use your portable sonar equipment for finding fish below the ice, just pour a little water on the ice and put the sonar's transducer in the water, flat against the ice. The inner cone shows 10-degree coverage while outer cone is 20 degrees.

Rods And Reels

You can hand-line in ice-time panfish or you can fish with a willow branch or a regular open-water rod. But handiest of all for ice fishing is probably a short, sensitive (graphite) rod—a 1 $\frac{1}{2}$- to 3-foot jiggle stick. It gets its name from the vertical jigging that ice fishermen do with it.

The shorter jiggle sticks work best in the tight quarters of a small ice shanty. Longer models serve well on open ice over deep water; they let you get a better hook-set. However, on open ice over shallow water, a short rod allows you to more easily watch fish in the hole. Some jiggle sticks are telescopic.

Some sticks offer fluorescent tips for easier bite detection, and some feature a built-in stand to keep it and the reel off the snow and ice.

Those rods equipped with cork handles are warmer for bare hands, and any rod used on open ice should have large line guides to prevent ice build-up problems. The stick can be coupled with one of several reel types—a small spincast or spinning reel, single action reel or line holder. Reels can be taped to the rod with electrical tape. It pays to bring several pre-rigged rods and reels along to save on fishing time.

Bite signalers—tip-ups—are more commonly used for large

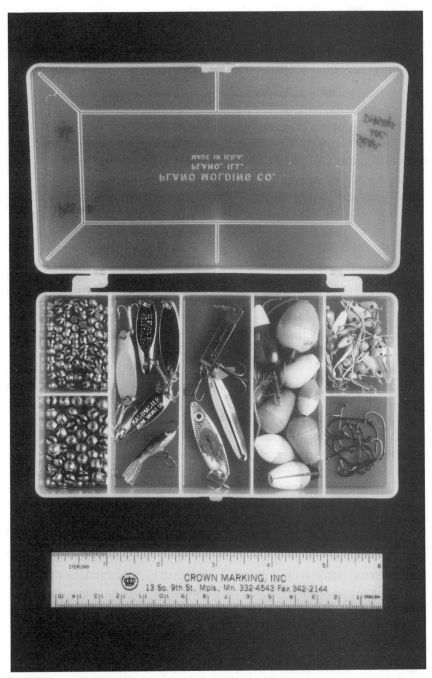

A pocket tacklebox loaded for ice fishing for panfish might include (left to right) small lead shot, a variety of jigging lures, small floats, ice flies (top right) and plain hooks.

Getting Equipped For Ice Fishing

gamefish; however, a few panfishermen use them, too. Scattered in an area, they may help to pinpoint panfish locations. For panfish, you need to use extra-sensitive models. These are more practical and less likely to get accidentally tripped during calm conditions out on the ice.

Line For Winter Fishing

Ice-fishing line should be somewhat tough—to handle the hole's jagged edges—yet thin so it's less visible to fish in the clear, winter water. High-quality $1/2$-pound to 4-pound test fools the most wary of winter panfish. (If you do use extra light line or leader like $1/2$ pound or 1 pound—such as fly tippet material—you'll need to use a reel with a smooth drag.) Six or 8-pound is often okay for panfish in deep water where the line isn't as visible. Special lines for easier handling in cold weather are now available, and these are available in blue so they're more visible on the ice, yet less visible to fish under the ice. Some anglers have long favored easily-seen and handled black braided 20- to 30-pound test line to which a few feet of light monofilament leader is attached.

Hooks And Baits

Panfish habitually eat small foods in winter, thus small, sharp hooks in the No. 16 to No. 6 range are tops. These hooks best accommodate small larvae—waxworms, maggots, goldenrod grubs, mousies, wigglers, mealworms—and small baitfish. It can pay to bring along several types of baits as some will work better than others. Hooks must be extra sharp (bring a file along) so that they easily penetrate the bait without injuring it too much. You may also need to file down the barb, especially when fishing tiny maggots on wispy line, for easier bait hooking and fish hooking.

The new fish attractants or natural-bait imitators such as artificial grubs can also help draw strikes; offerings with taste and odor catch extra panfish in winter. Also bring an assortment of different weights of split shot so you can keep the float's level right—barely at the surface—and to keep minnow action at the optimum level in the action zone.

Lures

It pays to stock an ice-fishing tacklebox with many sizes and types of lures, including colorful teardrops, ice jigs, ice flies (with

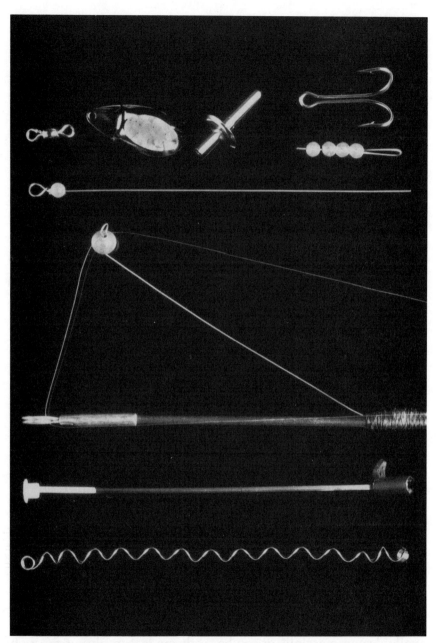

Spring bobbers offer unequalled sensitivity when attached to the tip of your ice-fishing rod. Make your own by using the wire and bead from a strip on spinner (top), or the spring from a ball point pen (bottom). Wrap the base of the wire to the rod with dacron fishing line, then coat the wrap with Superglue (center) and glue the bead to the eye of the wire. Also shown is a commercially made spring bobber.

Getting Equipped For Ice Fishing

or without miniature spinner blades) and vertically-fished minnow imitators and spoons. Jigs used in open water aren't often used under the ice, but they may work well, too.

This variety of tackle, usually tipped with bait, allows you to be ready for the different species encountered and for their ever-changing activity levels. Some of the lures have a rather stiff-type movement, possibly best for inactive panfish, while other ice lures dart, dive and quiver—possible hot baits for the hungrier biters.

Most ice jigs and flies for panfish weigh $1/200$ to $1/32$ ounce, with the tiniest ones imitating zooplankton. Panfish spoons weigh as little as $1/10$ ounce, but bring some heavier ones along in case you encounter deep perch and crappies. (You can also tie on a hook-less spoon above a leader and bait. The spoon attracts several species to the bait.)

Some ice lures are coated with soft plastic for a life-like feel, and lures are available in many colors, including phosphorescent colors for extra appeal in low light. Some lures come barbless, saving you the trouble of filing the barbs.

Some fishermen also like to keep some miniature snaps (not the larger snaps or swivel snaps) in the tackle box. One on the end of the line means lures can be easily changed without cutting line and re-tying. Small jigs and ice flies, however, work best when tied directly to the line.

Floats And Spring Bobbers

Winter panfish bites are often hardly noticeable, so the best ice-fishing floats are the tiniest possible, ones which barely hold up your bait. Ice should be kept off the floats, something easily accomplished when you use sponge rubber floats. Slip-bobbers and bobber stops are handy for deep-water fishing as long as they're kept ice-free. Even if you don't use a bobber, a bobber stop can be kept on the line. You can place it at water level and it will help you get back to the hot fishing depth after you reel a fish in.

A spring bobber is a length of springy wire attached to the rod, positioned over the rod's end or extending from it. It moves and indicates a bite more readily than the rod does. Spring bobbers are available commercially or can be easily made. Simply cut a 6-inch length of springy wire, such as guitar string. At one end, make a small loop to form the eye. Some like to thread on a red plastic bead at the eye so they notice bites more easily. Then, tape the other end to the rod so the eye end is even with or extended out from the rod tip. If you put it even with the rod tip, bend up the wire so the eye is a couple inches above the tip.

Other Gear

Miscellaneous gear to bring out on the ice include an insulated minnow bucket, a minnow scoop and an ice scoop to keep holes clear. Some scoops fit both purposes, and some also feature a small ice chisel on the handle end.

Also, a lunch box packed with some nutritious snacks and a thermos full of a hot coffee or juice can make the ice outing a more pleasant experience, keeping your energy up and tiding you over until that fish fry at home.

19

Ice Fishing Tactics For Sunfish, Crappies

While an orange sun climbs over the snowy horizon, announcing the morning's start of a panfish outing, you drill an ice hole, and it promptly gives up fat bluegill and, a minute later, a crappie. Finding both fish in the very same ice hole is common. The winter locations of these same-family species many times coincide. A heavy, mixed stringer can result from lowering a tiny ice fly tipped with a maggot or some other larva.

But, of course, for the best ice fishing catches, it pays to keep in mind the two fishes' different habits. Fortunately, today's ice fishermen have much more effective fish finding and catching techniques, compared to the methods of not many years ago.

Locating Ice-Time Sunfish

On many lakes, sunfish are the most common ice-fishing catch, and right after ice-up is a top time to catch them. Places you caught sunfish in summertime are often good early-winter locations. In fact, before the ice forms is a great time to find areas. You'll find bluegills elsewhere, but the best places are weedy points, bars and, especially, bays of just several feet deep or less. Big bluegills commonly lurk near the bases of the thick weeds, or if available, rocks, stumps and brush. Often overlooked in winter are small farm ponds. Again check for sunfish-holding cover, possibly near the pond's dam.

On a lake you've never fished, a bait shop operator may be able

Ice fishing for sunfish can provide some of the fastest action of the year, especially early and late in the winter season, as this fisherman in his portable shelter proves.

Ice Fishing Tactics For Sunfish, Crappies

to tell you the whereabouts of the bays and points. (Or if it's big bull bluegills you're after, the operator might be able to recommend a special lake.) If available, a lake map, of course, also helps locate top general structure, and once the ice forms, you can use a handline or, quicker yet, sonar to find the right depths. You can look for weeds or wood through the ice hole in clear water, or use sonar or a handline.

Some years, early-ice sunfishing starts before Halloween in the most-northerly reaches. For most anglers, though, it's around December or later. The main consideration is safe ice thickness: clear lake ice at least 2 inches thick is necessary to support the weight of one person; at least 3 inches for a few people widely separated, and about one foot for a car or light pickup. (Double these figures for slushy ice or weak dark ice. Also, river ice is generally weaker than lake ice.)

There's one exception to the safe-ice rule. An interesting brand of ice fishing can be enjoyed where docks or piers remain on the lake through the winter. Even if the ice is only an inch thick, you can walk out on the dock or pier (as long as it's not slippery) and break holes in the ice at various depths with a chisel or ax. The longer docks or piers offer a good selection of water depths as well as cover preferred by sunfish.

Mid- And Late-Winter Sunnies

After the ice gets thick, in mid-winter, sunfish may inhabit deeper water. However, the fish still hold near cover, maybe at a deep weedy or rocky drop-off or a rock pile. Such areas which are adjacent to big weedy bays may be hotspots. Late in the winter, the shallower water again may see sunfish activity. Try the same places you fished in early winter.

Catching Sunfish

Top sunfishing gear includes a jiggle stick, 1- to 4-pound line, and one of several lures or baits. Sunfish eat tiny foods in wintertime, so tiny, sharp hooks and little baits like waxworms or maggots can't be beat. Consider using two or more hooks on the line, if legal, for faster action, and though other colors work, too, ice jigs or flies colored yellow or white are good starting points. Spring bobbers or extra-sensitive dime-sized floats help you catch more light-biting sunfish.

Complete Angler's Library

These dandy bluegills all fell to an ice fly fished under a spring bobber on a light jigging stick. When you've got these kinds of bruisers to chase, winter is a lot of fun.

A sonar unit can quickly eliminate water with few or no sun-fish. Without sonar, a good way to find fish is to start fishing a foot or two below the surface. After just a minute, drop the bait a cou-ple feet, repeating this until you hit bottom. When you start to test-fish holes, you don't know what the mood of the sunfish will be. But, a tiny bait on 1-pound line should catch fish in most cases, so it's a good starting rig. You can always change later when you determine the fish's mood.

If multiple baits are legal, that will speed up the test-fishing process. If fishing with another angler, one can start fishing at the top, the other from the bottom. Or space yourselves many yards apart so you're doing something different.

Sunfish bites may be extremely light. If using a spring bobber, you'll need to keep the rod motionless some way. If an angler can't hold the rod still, he should put the rod on an ice-rod stand or other prop.

Even if you miss a fish's bite, you've found a good level to return the bait to. However, since you missed the bite, it might have been a reluctant fish, a hint that another lure or bait would work better under these conditions.

If there are no hits at all, it's time to move several yards away to new weeds or rocks that might harbor bluegills. You may need to move a dozen times during the day; there's no need to spend much time at any one spot if the fish aren't there.

Matching Bait To Mood

If the water's clear, it can pay to cover your head with a coat or canvas so you can look into nature's big aquarium below you and watch the fish's reactions to the baits. The sunfish will tell you what they specifically want.

Inactive sunnies may want just a single waxworm (or golden-rod grub or maggot) on a bare hook and 1- or 2-pound line. Active biters, however, might be more quickly nabbed with a larger (though still small) ice jig tipped with one or more of the larval baits available at your bait shop.

Try making slow circular motions with your rod tip, and experiment with other bait and lure movements. All sunfish are normally attracted by twitching the bait (or by a bait that provides movement, such as a wiggler). Jiggle the bait up and down often, particularly for hungry biters, though what triggers even the active fish to swallow the morsel is often the pause between twitches. If the sunnies are reluctant, use the tiny bait, tear it for extra smell, just occasionally jiggle it and keep it still most of the time. The fish won't want to bother with a busy bait.

To get a concentration of sunfish going, chumming the hole with some larval baits may work. If fishing gets hot, extra rigs—pre-rigged at home—are handy in case a line breaks or tangles.

Of course, once you're catching sunnies, it's important to get back to the right depth, especially if you're not using a sonar unit to determine the depth of your fishing bait and the sunfish. If you don't use a bobber, use some kind of marker on the line. A bobber stop or a rubber band will serve the purpose.

In certain situations you can catch great numbers of sunfish at night in summer, and ice-time sunnies can be caught at night, too.

Complete Angler's Library

This angler experiences the excitement of hoisting a hefty bluegill through a hole in the ice. During midwinter these fish bite light and eat little, but can be caught.

Ice Fishing Tactics For Sunfish, Crappies   259

Tying On A Leader Snell Hook

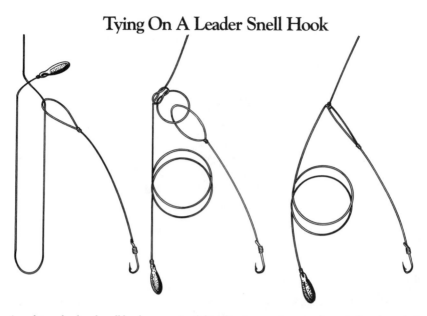

Attaching a leadered snell hook to your ice fishing line is easy. Just run the main line through the leader's loop, bring it around and tie a square knot over the leader loop, holding leader in place.

Other anglers prefer fishing in daytime. Sunfish may bite well the first part of morning and then in late afternoon, but they may bite well at midday, too, particularly under darker conditions.

Locating Ice-Time Crappies

In some regions, the most sought-after ice species is the crappie, which readily hits ice fishermen's offerings.

Generally, look for winter crappies to suspend near structure or cover, but their depth may vary widely. In frozen Mississippi River backwaters, crappies may swim in only two feet of water, while in a deep natural lake, crappies are commonly caught at 20 to 30 feet. However, as a general rule, many early winter crappies hover in rather shallow water, and they're near cover such as weedlines, weedy flats, brush, stumps, sunken boats and rock piles. In early winter, the bottom and mid-depths often lure crappies.

Additionally, enclosed heated crappie fishing docks are common on some Southern and Midwestern reservoirs. They're excellent fishing sites during unsafe early (or late) ice. For a small fee, you're in business; you can usually quickly find crappies around the docks' cover which is usually brush piles. Also, fishermen here who are experienced in fishing the dock may share fish catching information with first-timers.

Mid-Winter And Late-Winter Crappies

In mid-winter, cold weather may push crappies deep (it's warmer near the bottom in winter) particularly if there's forage for them. Consider fishing deep structure, such as along the edges of deep rock piles or deep drops. Now a sonar unit can be an immense help. Big-river crappies, though, commonly look for forage in the shallower backwaters in mid-winter.

In late winter, many fish move into shallower water again, toward future spawning areas. Also, low oxygen levels in some lakes (due to heavy ice and snow cover) causes crappies to swim into the more oxygen-rich water just beneath the ice or near stream inlets.

In any month, you can get a bait shop report to find out where exactly the crappies are hitting (or where the big-crappie lakes are), or you can watch for other crappie anglers on the ice. Crappie fans are sometimes out in droves, and you might join them. Lots of hole-drilling, ice-stomping anglers in one spot, though, can spook crappies. Try holes at likely depths, but a bit away from the crowd. Or, if the area is fished mainly during daytime, try it at night.

Test Fishing

Normally, successful crappie ice fishermen are extra mobile, testing several spots to find the specks. Simple, open-ice angling is tops if it's not too cold. If a shelter is used, a simple windbreak or lightweight canvas tent is usually best. Shelters improve your underwater visibility, too; you can see crappies take the bait and watch their reactions.

Test different sites with sonar or by test-fishing holes with multiple hooks or ice lures (if allowed) at different depths. Keep in mind crappies can be a bit spookier than bluegills, in shallower water at least, so it pays to be quiet. Sometimes, if you drill holes and come back an hour or more later after things calm down, the holes produce better. And, it's a good idea to use old ice holes, ones which haven't frozen over because there's less noise in opening them. Holes can be protected from freezing over covering them with a mound of snow.

Commonly, the choice ice-fishing baits prove to be crappie minnows such as fatheads or small shiners an inch and a half or so long, either hooked on an angled-shank No. 6 or No. 8 hook (with or without a tiny spinner blade) or on an ice lure such as a teardrop hook. The teardrop helps keep a minnow in place, making it easier for a crappie to take it. Hook the minnow on the back with the hook point facing toward the front of the minnow. Other tipping baits include worms, a single or several larvae, salmon eggs or a squirt of bottled panfish attractant.

If the fish are active, the color might not make much difference, but sometimes a certain hue like yellow or chartreuse takes the most fish. And, as with other fish, if they're finicky, more crappies might be caught with something tiny and less mobile such as a larval bait or miniature minnow on an ice fly. For wildly feeding specklesides, however, a big crappie minnow with only a single split shot or a jigging lure—something that moves around—is

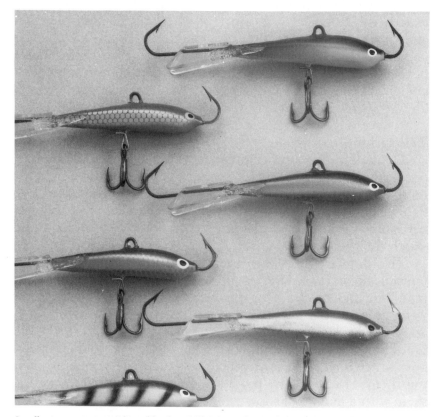

Small minnow-imitating lures like these Nils Master Jiggers from Acme Tackle can be effective in ice fishing for panfish. And, artificials can catch fish faster than live minnow rigs.

Complete Angler's Library

Most winter crappies probably are taken on minnows. It's probably the best all-round bait, but if the crappies seem to be finicky, try putting a larva on 1-pound-test line.

Ice Fishing Tactics For Sunfish, Crappies

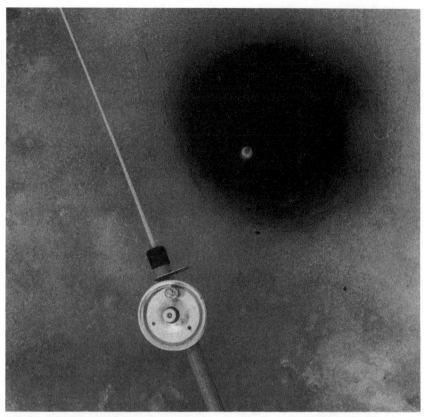

Use the smallest possible float so that it will present very little resistance when the bait is taken by light-biting sunfish. If they feel resistance, they may spit the bait out before they're hooked.

often more attractive. Jiggle any crappie offerings just a bit every 30 seconds or so, then let it rest.

One- to 4-pound line or leader (on the end of some easily seen and handled dark-braided line) gets the wariest of the fish. If you don't want to use a tiny float, you should use a jiggle stick that is extra sensitive or one fitted with a spring bobber, but remember that a spring bobber is only effective when combined with the lightest lures and line.

When using a float, you don't necessarily need a rod for crappies. You can rig up with the line still on the spool it came on. Set in the snow by the ice hole, the spool revolves easily when a fish pulls. In a shanty, you can hang the spool on a nail on the wall above the hole. A reel, though, can prevent tangles, a common occurrence when the crappie fishing gets hot.

If you ice one crappie, you know there's probably a school below you. It's crucial to get an offering back down immediately. If they're frantically feeding, it's wise to have another rod rigged up with a small jigging minnow-imitator because using live bait eats up fishing time. Snap up the line so the lure darts to one side, then pause to let it fall back to center, and repeat. Alternatives are a jigging spoon or a strip of tough-skinned fish meat on a hook or ice lure, maybe dipped in panfish attractant. Anyway you do it, this quick-type fishing helps keep the crappies close and interested.

It helps to get back to the same depth each time. If you've caught a crappie that's bigger than the others, that fish's depth is the one you want to return to. Crappies often travel with same-size fish, but some crappie schools have mixed sizes. The big slabs may be at any depth, but during active feeding, they may claim the area at the school's top where they can get the best shot at minnows. There's a definite pecking order among crappies.

The best time of day to ice fish for crappies? Some anglers go for the early morning bites, and dark-water lakes can provide fine midday action. Overall, however, most fish are probably taken in late afternoon. Also, on clear lakes especially, a fisherman shouldn't overlook night fishing. Angling from a lantern-lit shanty can sometimes provide some fast icing of winter crappies.

20

Ice Fishing
For Perch

I ce fishing for perch is a sport that's seen steady growth in recent years. Why? Because many American anglers have found that not only can it be a comfortable business, given good clothing or an ice shanty, it's also productive. Sometimes *very* productive. Studies by fisheries biologists have shown that the catch per hour ratio is higher for ice fishing than at any other time of year. And perch taken from water little above freezing are at their best in the skillet. Good reasons for risking some discomfort and chilblains.

Finding perch beneath the ice can often be an easy business on large, popular lakes. Hotspots are traditional and well known, and any bait shop can give directions to the nearest. Then it's a matter of trudging out to where as many as 100 anglers may be already congregated, boring holes and dropping lines.

It pays to stroll around a bit first, rather than stopping at random. If a few anglers out on one fringe have goodly piles of fish and others have only a few, then set up shop there. And if nothing much is going on anywhere, either head for another place or start cutting holes off to one side of the main pack, until you find success and fish!

Keep in mind that schools move around and if they find a good food source a short distance from their usual feeding grounds, they'll gather there. A shift of as little as 10 yards may find them. Whatever the choice, and whatever your location, the best action is still likely to be early and late most days, so it pays to get there at

Perch like this are worth scouting for, and when you find them, you'll usually find them schooled together by size. When you catch a large perch, stay in that immediate area.

Ice Fishing For Perch

first light, or stay until nearly dark for bigger catches.

If there are only a few or no other anglers, then you'll have to search for the schools and that can take time, even several trips. But a map of the bottom will reduce both the odds and effort. Most, probably all, state fish and game departments will have contour maps of their major lakes, with depths, fish structure, drop-offs, islands, parking lots and access ramps, and they're available either free or for a very nominal cost from their publications sections. Such maps are worth their weight in perch fillets.

Look for reefs, remnants of weed beds, underwater ledges or any other structure, and fish near them. Seek out hard-rock bottom when it's available, and if there are boulders, so much the better. Such places offer both food and a certain amount of protection, and they'll draw perch. Keep in mind, though, that on some lakes like Minnesota's Mille Lacs, for example, perch often leave hard bottom in mid-winter to range over deep mud flats, seeking insect larvae that burrow there. No rule is iron clad.

Small portable electronic depthfinders are a quick way of finding fish on lakes that are unknown to you. A few anglers have learned to bore very shallow holes in the ice and fill them with water for a quick look at what's below. This method saves plenty of hole boring and setting up time since, if no fish are down there, you can just move on. On colder days when the water freezes, use a non-metal container filled partially with water and antifreeze solution and place it in the shallow hole you've made in the ice. The method doesn't always work, particularly on old ice that might be filled with debris and air pockets, so an alternative on fairly thin ice or if you're carrying along a gas-powered auger is to punch a hole clear through, insert the business end of your fish finder, then do some checking below.

A depthfinder will also show bottom structure that an angler might be seeking, perhaps a reef that is known to be in the general area. It is even handier when fish are holding above bottom, which they sometimes do. Fishing six inches up when the fish are five feet higher explains a lot of wasted fishing trips, something that won't happen with a portable fish locator.

There are bound to be situations, especially on small Northern lakes, where you're lacking a fish locator, have no maps, no one else is fishing, and you've no idea where the perch might be hiding. If that's the case, try to at least get a starting point from a local

Perch contests make winters seem a little bit shorter, especially on lakes where perch this size swim. Contests show what size perch you might expect to find in a lake.

bait shop—east, west, north or south sides of the lake. Then, start at medium depths and work deeper as the morning progresses, or start deep and move toward the shallows as the afternoon wanes. You may have to dig a lot of holes, but you'll eventually find fish.

When you've found a productive spot, the trick is to return to that exact same spot another time. If you have a compass with degree markings, it's easy to find it again by triangulation, taking a degree reading on two separate fixed, prominent landmarks on shore. Then, write down these markings on a rough map of the shoreline. If you don't have a compass or one of the commercial triangulation finders on the market, don't despair. If you can line up two fixed, prominent points on each line of sight, then with a total of four points you can find the spot where the two lines of sight meet. The major difficulty is finding a second, more distant landmark on each sight line, particularly where land abutting the shoreline is flat.

Luckily, most serious perch lakes are well known and well used, so the basic tactic of joining the crowd will be enough to find good fish most times. It's in the catching that an average angler will succeed or fail. Luckily, that's no real problem either, given diligence and a willingness to work for a nice dinner.

On any lake, a fair proportion of anglers are social animals.

Ice Fishing For Perch

They're out there to catch fish, but they're also out to have fun and enjoy a welcome break from work and family duties. So they'll bore holes, drop lines, watch them a few minutes, then wander off to converse, drink coffee and see what others are doing, keeping only an occasional eye on their own lines. That's not the way to fill a bucket with perch.

You can fish spreaders or tandem rigs (the latter are better), use brightly colored little tear drop-shaped ice spoons, or add red or yellow beads above the hooks as an attractant. Whatever you personally prefer. But do remember that floats should be barely big enough to hold up the bait. Perch can be gentle biters at times, and a large float won't react much when a light-finned customer bites, and its resistance usually causes the fish to drop the bait.

Some anglers go even further when fishing in ice shanties and

Panfish ice-fishing gear includes portable one-man shelter from Winter Fishing Systems, and portable flasher-type depthfinder. Now you're ready to find and catch fish!

Complete Angler's Library

Think portable to find fish. The two-man shelter (left) from KL Industries, Muskegon, Mich., folds compactly, as does the Fish Trap from Winter Fishing Systems, Fridley, Minn.

use no float at all. Instead, they'll tie their lines to the ceiling, fold a loop in the line at eye level, and attach a rubber band to the loop's top and bottom, adding a small tie of colored yarn. Even a perch biting with infinite care will move that rubber band and yarn at least a fraction of an inch, and then he can be pulled in hand over hand.

It's important to keep in mind that the bait must move, at least occasionally. Perch are attuned to movement, which to their half-frozen brains means something edible. Jig the bait occasionally, using up and down movements of the rod tip that should measure no more than a few inches. Where the law allows, fall into a rhythm using two rods. Jig one a few seconds, then let it rest while you jig the other. Bites usually come during the pause as perch suddenly recognize the object as food. Leaving the bait dead in the water will produce only perch that happen to pass very closely to the bait and that won't happen often.

Minnows are the traditional bait in winter just as in summer, and probably 90 percent of all anglers head forth with a bucket of shiners or fatheads. Most days they'll work fine. Use very small minnows on a tear-drop-shaped ice spoon, a plain hook with or

Sensitive Bite Detector

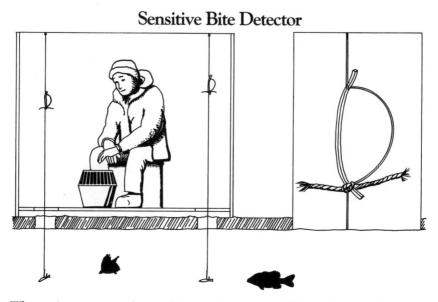

When you're trying to watch a couple lines for those shy panfish bites, this trick will help a lot. With a piece of a rubber band, tie both ends to the line so the line forms a loop; then, tie a piece of yarn or ribbon to the bottom knot. When the shy bite occurs, the yarn will move just slightly.

without a colored bead, or a smaller-sized jigging spoon with a minnow impaled on the spoon's treble hook when perch are running larger than usual. And don't forget that in a lake loaded with jumbo perch, the bigger minnows will often produce bigger fish. A 5-inch perch isn't interested in a 3-inch minnow unless he's unusually ambitious or unusually hungry.

On many occasions, other baits will actually work better than minnows, and that holds especially true when the lake swarms with forage fish. A small ice fly with a waxworm or maggot on the hook has taken many a hungry perch, and mayfly larvae are excellent offerings wherever bait shops have them. Lots of perch are taken, too, on ice spoons and mealworms or mousies. They're insect eaters at heart, and as long as those small spoons or flies are jigged occasionally, they should catch fish.

Needless to say, there are plenty of refinements evolved by old time fishermen to (hopefully) increase their catch, and some of them even work. For example, in traditional hotspots that have been producing at least modest catches for weeks, you can often draw more perch to your particular hole by perforating a can of sardines packed in oil, then lowering it on a string to bottom, allowing that rich oil to ooze in all directions. The fishy odor seems to draw perch, especially when there's at least a little current in the lake. Don't forget to pull the can back up when you're done.

Some anglers fishing over a dark bottom in known hotspots have been known to drop handfuls of silver-gray driveway gravel, or crushed up clam shells to make a light spot that may attract curious perch. Others might "chum," where legal, or even try mechanical "fish callers" or blobs of commercial attractant. There's little question that a squirt of fish-flavored oil, or a drop or two added to a bait will help make up the mind of a reluctant feeder.

Ice fishing for perch can be summed up in a few simple rules. Find the right spot, use the right equipment and bait and jig. If perch are there, you should catch some.

Index

A

American perch, 170
Anchors, 66
Attached sinkers, 30
Augers, 242

B

Bail trigger, 26
Baitcasting reels, 26
Bait, 16, 42-52, 72, 120, 162, 173, 193,
    198-199, 215, 232, 250, 271-272
  caddisworms, 46
  catalpa worms, 46
  clams, 50
  crayfish, 48, 50
  crickets, 46, 50, 72
  doll flies, 193
  earthworms, 44-45, 50, 72, 232
  fathead minnows, 42-44
  frogs, 49
  gallworms, 46
  goldenrod grubs, 46
  grasshoppers, 46
  grubs, 50
  hellgrammites, 46
  katydids, 46
  larval baits, 45-46
  leeches, 48
  maggots, 46, 50
  mayfly nymphs, 46
  mealworms, 46
  minnows, 42-44, 50, 162, 173, 271-272
  pork rinds, 50
  shiners, 44
  shrimp, 48-49, 50
  stone fly nymphs, 46
  tent caterpillars, 46
  threadfin shad, 44
  waxworms, 46
Bank sinkers, 32
Bantam sunfish, 97
Barbels, 229
Barbless hooks, 30
Barfish, 214
Barrel sinkers, 33
Bass-casting sinkers, 32
Batteries, 66
Bead-chain sinkers, 32
Beaver lodges, 225
Bell sinkers, 32
Black bullhead, 228
Black crappie, 128-133
Blue catfish, 230, 235
Bluegill/bassin' connection, 76-77

Bluegills, 72-77
  color, 72-74
  life span, 76
  size, 74-76
  spawning behavior, 76
  weight, 74
Boat docks, 105-106
Boat fishing, 201-203
Boats, 37-41, 58-67, 141-142, 164, 167,
  191, 221, 246, 257
  anchors, 66
  batteries, 66
  canoes, 60, 221
  downriggers, 167, 191
  electric motors, 64-65
  johnboats, 60-62
  life jackets, 67
  livewells, 62
  mini bass boat, 60
  motors, 62-65
  outboard motors, 62-64
  paper graph sonar, 41
  semi-v hull boats, 60
  sonar, 37-41, 65-66, 164, 246, 257
  trailers, 65
  video display sonar, 41
Bobbers, 28, 33-37, 141-142, 252-253
Bream, 70, 72
Bridges, 106
Brown bullheads, 228
Bucktail jigs, 53
Bullet sinkers, 33
Bullheads, 226-235

C
Caddisworms, 46
Cane poles, 22
Canoes, 60, 221
Casting bubbles, 36
Casting rods, 20-22
Catalpa worms, 46
Catfish, 226-237
Channel catfish, 230, 235
Chisel, 240
Clams, 50
Clinch sinkers, 32
Cover, 54, 100, 115, 117-118, 119, 121, 254
Crankbaits, 56, 200, 225
Crappies, 42, 44, 50, 52, 53, 126-167,
  260-265

  black, 126, 128-133
  habitat, 138-141
  suspended, 163-166
  white, 126
Crayfish, 48, 50
Cricket cage, 46
Crickets, 46, 50, 72
Current breaks, 220

D
Deep water, 118-121
Dipsey sinkers, 32
Doll flies, 193
Dollar sunfish, 97
Downrigging, 167, 191
Drifting, 158-159, 186, 203
Drills, 242, 244

E
Ear flaps, 73, 78
Earthworms, 44-45, 50, 72, 232
Egg sinkers, 33
Electric motors, 64-65
Equipment, 20-41, 161-162, 187-188
  anchors, 66
  augers, 242
  baitcasting reels, 26
  batteries, 66
  boats, 58-67
  cane poles, 22
  casting rods, 20-22
  chisel, 240
  drills, 242, 244
  electric motors, 64-65
  fiberglass rods, 20-22
  flashers, 37-41
  fly rods, 23-24
  graphite rods, 20-22
  johnboats, 60-62
  life jackets, 67
  liquid crystal display sonar, 41
  livewells, 62
  markers, 201-203
  minnow buckets, 44
  motors, 62-65
  mini bass boat, 60
  outboard motors, 62-64
  paper graph sonar, 41
  polarized sunglasses, 115
  pole reels, 27

reels, 24-28, 248-250
rods, 20-24, 248-250
semi-v hull boats, 60
sonar, 37-41, 65-66, 164, 246, 257
spincasting reels, 24
spinning reels, 24-26
tackle box, 56-57
trailers, 65
video display sonar, 41
European bobbers, 36-37

F
Fathead minnows, 42-44
Fiberglass rods, 20-22
Fixed bobbers, 34
Fixed sinkers, 30
Flashers, 37-41
Flat bullheads, 229
Flathead catfish, 235-237
Fliers, 97
Fly lures, 56
Fly rods, 23-24
Food, 24, 130, 159
Frogs, 49

G
Gallworms, 46
Gear ratios, 24, 26
Goggle eyes, 218
Gold bass, 214
Goldenrod grubs, 46
Graphite rods, 20-22
Grasshopper cage, 46
Grasshoppers, 46
Green sunfish, 88-91
  habitat, 88, 90
  range, 88
  size, 89
Grubs, 50
Guides (rods), 22
Guinea perch, 97

H
Habitat, 100-101, 112
Hair jigs, 53
Hellgrammites, 46
Hooks, 28, 29-30, 53, 234, 250
  barbless, 30
  sharpening, 30

size, 29-30
Hybrid sunfish, 94-95

I
Ice fishing, 240-273
  bait, 250
  clothing, 246
  drills, 240-244
  hooks, 250
  line, 250
  lures, 250-252
  reels, 248
  rods, 248
  shelters, 244-246
  sonar, 246
  tip-ups, 248-250

J
Jack perch, 170
Jigs, 52-54, 120, 140, 191-193, 199-200, 215
  color, 54
  sizes, 53-54
Johnboats, 60-62

K
Katydids, 46

L
Lake perch, 170
Lakes, 138-153
Larval baits, 45-46
Leeches, 48
Life jackets, 67
Lighted bobbers, 36
Line, 27-28, 112, 250
  color, 28
  fly, 28
  stretchability, 28
  weight, 26, 28, 112, 157
Liquid crystal display sonar, 41
Livewells, 62
Longear sunfish, 84-88
  color, 84
  habitat, 86, 87
  range, 86
  size, 86-87
Lures, 16, 52-54, 56, 102, 113-114, 120,
  140, 191-193, 199-200, 215, 225, 250-252
  bucktail jigs, 53

crankbaits, 56, 200, 225
fly lures, 56
hair jigs, 53
ice fishing lures, 250-252
jigs, 52-54, 120, 140, 191-193, 199-200, 215
spoons, 56
topwater plugs, 56

M
Maggots, 46, 50
Marabou-bodied jig, 52, 53
Markers, 201-203
Mayfly nymphs, 46
Mealworms, 46
Mini bass boat, 60
Minnow buckets, 44
Minnows, 42-44, 50, 162, 173, 271-272
Motors, 62-65
Mousies, 46

N
Night fishing, 160-163, 211

O
Orange-spotted sunfish, 97
Outboard motors, 62-64
Oxbow lakes, 221
Ozark bass, 218

P
Paper graph sonar, 41
Pencil bobbers, 36
Perch, 42, 50, 52, 266-273
pH, 129
Pier fishing, 191, 194-200
Plankton, 159
Plastic jig, 52-53
Polarized sunglasses, 115
Pole reels, 27
Ponds, 114-118
Pork rinds, 50
Presentation, 102, 141-142
Pumpkinseeds, 78, 91-93
Pyramid sinkers, 32

Q
Quill bobbers, 36

R
Raccoon perch, 170
Redbreast sunfish, 80-83
color, 81
ear flaps, 82
habitat, 82-83
range, 82
spawning, 83
Redear sunfish, 77-79
color, 78
grinding teeth, 79
habitat, 80
range, 79
size, 79
spawning, 80
Redeyes, 218
Reels, 24-28, 248-250
bail trigger, 26
baitcasting reels, 26
gear ratios, 24, 26
ice fishing reels, 248
pole reels, 27
spincasting reels, 24
spinning reels, 24-26
Reservoirs, 138-153
Ringed perch, 170
Rio Grande perch, 97
River perch, 170
Rivers, 138-153, 219
Roanoke bass, 218
Rock bass, 216-221
Rock ledges, 220-221
Rods, 20-24, 248-250
cane poles, 22
casting rods, 20-22
fiberglass rods, 20-22
fly rods, 23-24
graphite rods, 20-22
guides (rods), 22
ice fishing rods, 248
Rubber-core sinkers, 32

S
Sand bass, 210
Sacramento perch, 97
Saugers, 170
Semi-v hull boats, 60
Shadow bass, 218

Shiners, 44
Shrimp, 48-49, 50
Silver bass, 210
Sinkers, 28, 30-33
Sliding sinkers, 30, 33
Slip bobbers, 34
Slip sinkers, 30, 33
Sloughs, 221
Sonar, 37-41, 65-66, 164, 246, 257
  flashers, 37-41
  ice fishing use, 246
  liquid crystal display sonar, 41
  paper graph sonar, 41
  transducers, 37, 167
  video display sonar, 41
Spawning, 76, 98, 102-104, 114, 115,
  130-132, 136-137, 145-148, 196
Spincasting reels, 24
Spinnerbaits, 54-56
Spinning reels, 24-26
Split shot, 30-32
Spoons, 56
Spotted sunfish, 93-94
Spreaders, 188-189, 270
Stone fly nymphs, 46
Streak, 214
Streams, 121-123
Stripe, 214
Striped bass, 208
Striped perch, 170
Structure, 119-120, 140, 184-186, 219, 221,
  268
Sunfish, 45, 50, 52, 70-123
  bluegills, 72-77
  feeding levels, 100
  redbreasts, 81-83
  redears, 77-80
  predators, 76-77
Swamps, 221

T
Tackle box, 56-57
Tandem hook rigs, 188, 189-190, 270
Tent caterpillars, 46
Terminal tackle, 28-29, 188
Thermocline, 118-119
Threadfin shad, 44
Time of day, 100, 232
Topwater plugs, 56

Trailers, 65
Transducers, 37, 167
Trolling, 166, 190
Trolling rigs, 190
Trolling sinkers, 32
Trotlining, 237

V
Vertical fishing, 156-157
Video display sonar, 41

W
Walking sinkers, 32
Walleyes, 170
Warmouth, 216-218, 221-225
Water clarity, 110-114, 130, 140
Water depth, 118-121
Water pH, 129
Water temperature, 76, 103, 104, 109, 115,
  129, 145, 152-153, 154
Waxworms, 46
Weather, 105-109, 112, 142-145, 148-150,
  154, 156, 196-198, 203-205, 212
Weedbeds, 106-108, 117, 153, 232
White bass, 42, 55, 208-213
  jump fishing, 211
  night fishing, 211
  range, 210
  schooling habits, 210, 211
  size, 210
  spawning, 210
White crappie, 133-137
Wind, 157-160
Worm bedding, 45
Worm boxes, 45

Y
Yellow bass, 208, 214-215
Yellow bullhead, 228
Yellow perch, 170-205, 214
  color, 170
  food, 176, 193
  habitat, 172, 174, 180, 184-185
  range, 170-172
  schooling habits, 176-179
  size, 172, 179
  spawning habits, 175-176
Yellowjack, 214